Claiming Resurrection
in the Dying Church

Claiming Resurrection in the Dying Church

Freedom beyond Survival

Anna B. Olson

WESTMINSTER
JOHN KNOX PRESS
LOUISVILLE · KENTUCKY

First edition
Published by Westminster John Knox Press
Louisville, Kentucky

16 17 18 19 20 21 22 23 24 25—10 9 8 7 6 5 4 3 2 1

Unless otherwise indicated, Scripture quotations are from the New Revised Standard Version of the Bible, copyright © 1989 by the Division of Christian Education of the National Council of the Churches of Christ in the U.S.A., and are used by permission.

Scripture quotations marked NIV are from *The Holy Bible, New International Version.* Copyright © 1973, 1978, 1984, 2011 by Biblica, Inc.® Used by permission. All rights reserved worldwide.

Book design by Sharon Adams
Cover design by Allison Taylor

Library of Congress Cataloging-in-Publication Data

Names: Olson, Anna B.
Title: Claiming resurrection in the dying church : freedom beyond survival / Anna B. Olson.
Description: Louisville, KY : Westminster John Knox Press, 2016.
Identifiers: LCCN 2015036793 | ISBN 9780664261177 (alk. paper)
Subjects: LCSH: Church renewal--United States. | Resurrection.
Classification: LCC BV600.3 .O425 2016 | DDC 262.001/7--dc23 LC record available at http://lccn.loc.gov/2015036793

♾ The paper used in this publication meets the minimum requirements of the American National Standard for Information Sciences—Permanence of Paper for Printed Library Materials, ANSI Z39.48-1992.

Most Westminster John Knox Press books are available at special quantity discounts when purchased in bulk by corporations, organizations, and special-interest groups. For more information, please e-mail SpecialSales@wjkbooks.com.

Contents

Acknowledgments

First thanks go to the people of St. Mary's Mariposa in Los Angeles for inviting me into your story and supporting this telling of it. Thanks also to the other congregations that have shaped my priesthood: the other St. Mary's (Manhattanville), Holy Faith, Trinity, and St. Luke's.

I am deeply grateful for the friends, colleagues, and family that have supported me at every turn and have helped me hone my reflections and ideas over the years. I am not sure I'm accomplished enough to merit a ten-page acknowledgment section that lists everyone by name and role. Hopefully, you know who you are.

Thank you to the Louisville Institute for the Pastoral Study Project Grant that provided space for this project to happen and especially for the winter seminar that inspired me to think that I could actually write a book.

Thank you to Mount Calvary and Ghost Ranch for being quiet and holy places to think, pray, and write. Thank you to Caffé Vita for being my writing spot close to home. I repent of all the mean things I ever said about hipster coffee shops.

Thank you to the Episcopal Church Foundation Vital Practices team for inviting me to blog and for inspiring me to think creatively about church on a regular basis.

Thank you to Westminster John Knox Press for taking a

chance on this first-time author and to Bob Ratcliff for guiding me through the process.

Thank you to everyone who read drafts, offered feedback, removed commas, and encouraged me to get this done!

Thanks be to God for the life of Malcolm Boyd, without whose spiritual direction and friendship I could not have even begun to write.

Introduction

This is a love letter to the dying church: an invitation to take stock of where we are and turn toward the center of the Christian story.

If you have opened a book with "dying church" in the title, it is probably because you already have some doubts about survival prospects for your church, or the church as a whole. Your congregation may be facing imminent closure. It may have an endowment that could keep it going years after the aging congregation has gone to its rest. It may be OK for now but attracting few new people. It may have an immediate sense of itself as dying or no sense at all. But you see the signs that the whole institutional project of the twentieth-century American church is on its way out; you see that your congregation, sooner or later, will be swept along with that wave of dying.

Maybe you are a lifelong member of your local church, and you have seen the pews gradually empty, your children and the children of your peers drift off. Maybe you are a newly ordained pastor, discovering that the place to which you brought your hopes and high expectations is at the end of its life. Maybe you are part of your congregation's leadership team and under tremendous pressure to come up with the right mission statement and the right strategic plan before the savings run out, and it's "last one out turn off the lights." Maybe you are an experienced pastor who

1

can't figure out why the things that used to work don't anymore, and you are starting to suspect that all the church growth formulas and products you have been sold are so much snake oil. Maybe you are a denominational leader, and you realize that many of the congregations in your purview are dying. It is getting late for turnaround strategies in many places.

The new millennium has been a wild ride for the U.S. church. The death of the church has been predicted, proclaimed, and pronounced. And now we are living it. Dying church is not as glamorous as it sounds in a manifesto nor as apocalyptic as it appears from crashing statistics. Here is what it looks like from where I stand: death comes one person, one beloved tradition, and one chunk of the roof at a time, a genteel crumbling that is more sad than dramatic. Dying congregations have tried just about everything, grasping after growth and renewal strategies with the panic-driven strength of drowning swimmers. We have looked on with not a little envy as newly planted churches shed the burdens and complications of the past. We look out on changed and changing neighborhoods and hang on to increasingly motley mixes of faithful people.

The fears of the historic church are not just monsters under the bed. We fear that we are at the end of an era, and we are. We fear that we have not yet seen the worst that the crumbling of the twentieth-century church has to offer, and we have not. We fear that things are falling apart faster and faster. They are. There is much loss still ahead. The last generation that upheld the historic churches is still to be lost. Most of our congregations have run out of time for renewal, if that was ever a realistic possibility; we are well past the possibility of gentle transition by which new generations gracefully fill our churches without cataclysmic change. The certainty that we will have neighbors looking to be "churched"—eager to commit to regular Sunday worship if only we can find ways to engage them—is a mirage.

We know all these things, but every fiber of our beings, every element of our institutional structures and every value of our culture push us away from the point of reckoning. I caught a glimpse the other day of one of the endless parade of preschool

TV shows. A character was frustrated, and his friends were looking on. Finally, he flopped down in defeat. A deathly silence fell over the watching crowd. Someone asked, "You're not . . . *giving up?*" A collective gasp went up. The animated friends began to chant. "Don't give up, don't give up." Giving up has become the unforgivable sin—worse than hitting, spitting, or using bad words and less developmentally defensible than refusing to share. Whatever you do, don't give up.

What if we give up? What if we concede that we don't know what to do with the current moment, or most of the last twenty years, and certainly not the next twenty? What if we admit that our congregations in their familiar forms will be gone in twenty years, or ten? What if we acknowledge that what we've been able to hang on to is slipping from our grasp?

> When Jesus had received the wine, he said, "It is finished." Then he bowed his head and gave up his spirit. (John 19:30)

What if we give up? Stop trying to pull ourselves out of the grave by our own bootstraps? What if we give up the idea that our hard work will be rewarded by a shining church and put our faith in the promise that the path to resurrection is through death? What if we let go of the idolatrous idea that God wants all human religious endeavors to thrive and trust that God is "making all things new"? The collective gasp may well become a sigh of relief. Becoming a congregation that tells the truth may be a great liberation. Some people will be angry, defiant, blame the quitters. But others will stand up taller, freed from the burden of carrying the lie.

Giving up does not have to mean locking the doors and going home. If God is not finished, we are not either. There is more for us: more life, more hope. But we are freed from knowing the shape it will take. We are freed from the daunting task of birthing the new with only our own waning strength. We begin to face the future with freedom and faith rather than fear and the weight of failure.

Giving up on success frees us. We are free to measure the

fruits of our ministry not by the marks of longevity, affluence, and popularity but rather by the mark set by Jesus: love of God and neighbor. If our churches cease striving to be full and flush, we can strive to be places where we and our neighbors practice welcoming and being welcomed, forgiving and being forgiven, loving and being loved. We can live fully in whatever time we have left, claiming our place in the sacred story of death and resurrection. Relinquishing our claim on survival, we can walk toward death in faith and hope, offering all that we have left to a God fully capable of doing a new thing in our neighborhoods and our communities. In short, we can be who we were always meant to be.

This book is for and about historic churches. By historic, I don't mean listed on a register somewhere or necessarily made of stone with a tall steeple and "architectural significance." Historic churches have some history in their neighborhoods and communities. They have served at least one full generation and are now living beyond the generation that they were planted to serve. While in most cases they were founded to meet the needs of a culturally particular and relatively homogeneous group, they now find themselves physically rooted in places that have changed beyond what that first generation could readily imagine.

This definition of historic may sound awfully Californian to my sisters and brothers elsewhere. In my defense, I will say only that the world is changing with increasingly California-like speed these days, even in places where it usually takes more than a generation to become historic. Being a historic church is different from being a church in its first generation. Generational shifts are messy, and church gets messier and messier as it attempts to serve in the midst of change. The generational and cultural range of the congregation grows over time, sometimes even as the congregation shrinks. Competing claims on the church's attention and focus intensify. Commuters and neighbors live in increasingly different worlds. Whether the church has served fifty or three hundred years, it is no longer the church it was when it started. The speed with which historic churches are called to reinvent themselves is often inversely proportional to the speed with which they are able to move.

This is not one more church growth book. It contains no promises. I do not know what will happen to my dying church, much less yours. I don't have the formula that will save you from death, the right prescription that will sustain you for ten years, twenty years, thirty years. I don't believe that all of our churches will survive, not even all the "good ones" who are trying hard to be faithful. Growth programs that promise results, measure faith by size, bind resurrection in institutions, and blame the faithful for the changing world have little good news for our churches. They lure us with promises of success when our faith calls for a willingness to die. Jesus' ministry was a failure by all the measures of church growth. He went from drawing crowds of thousands to struggling to hang on to his own inner circle of disciples. He went from raging popularity to ignominy.

Tolstoy famously began the novel *Anna Karenina*, "All happy families are alike; each unhappy family is unhappy in its own way." The same could be said for dying churches. Each one has its own trajectory, its own manifestation of the broad pattern of church decline. It is easy to become so isolated in the dying process that each of us imagines our story to be utterly unique. We imagine that we may be the only ones who have failed in quite this way. This book invites you to have some perspective and to find some company. We are in this together, and we are part of something large and sweeping—a reorganization of our society and our faith that affects all churches and goes well beyond the church.

The stories in this book come from my ministry, mostly from my recent years in the heart of Los Angeles at St. Mary's Episcopal Church. St. Mary's is a historic Japanese American church founded in 1907 when the neighborhood was called Uptown and was home to many Japanese immigrants. A century later it finds itself again in the midst of an immigrant neighborhood, now called Koreatown: majority Latino with a substantial and growing Korean population. When I arrived in 2011, St. Mary's was already deep into the painful process of realizing that its hoped-for future as a church for successive generations of Japanese

American families with ancestral roots in Uptown was probably not going to happen. While few St. Mary's members would be happy to describe the church as dying, the congregation's grief and disappointment are palpable. We lose one member after another who carries the story and history of what the church has meant to a community that has suffered and cared for one another. The descendants of St. Mary's founders have scattered to suburbs that are geographically and culturally far from the old neighborhood; fewer and fewer members of the younger generations of St. Mary's historic families pick up church where their elders left off.

St. Mary's has had to dig deep into its past, discovering an identity that goes beyond the sacred story of a particular ethnic community: it is an entry point for new immigrants, a place that loves children, and a place of refuge for those who have been left out and pushed out by the surrounding culture. I am privileged to serve in a brave place, one that is letting go of its hard-fought hopes for its future, more or less embracing the neighbors who have ventured in the doors and trying to muster a spirit of adventure for an unknown future.

I have been a parish priest for fourteen years in and around Los Angeles, all in churches that have seen generations come and go, both in the congregation and in their neighborhoods. The churches I have served are canaries in the mineshaft of church decline: smaller, urban congregations in tough, fast-changing, impoverished, diverse neighborhoods. With no glee, I imagine that our fate foretells that of more prosperous congregations in easier settings. Our churches feel the impact of the shifts in culture and generation more immediately, more harshly. As is the case for the people in the communities we serve, there is not much to cushion our fall—not much commonality with and among neighbors, not much money, not many resources designed for our contexts. We live from crisis to crisis, and in the midst of this madness, we are told that our problems would be solved if only we formed more small groups, put up better signs and websites, spent more on technology, and spiffed up our music.

It wasn't easy for me to claim my vocation as a priest in the dying church. I spent years believing that it was my job, and the job of the congregations I served, to ensure a future for ourselves. I read books, went to conferences, wrote mission statements, took surveys, and formed task forces all in the service of church survival. I had some pretty good ideas. I tried to stay positive and always have another strategy in my pocket. I served faithful congregations with real spiritual gifts, full of people who wanted to see their churches survive and thrive. I tried hard to serve them well. When I ran out of ideas for securing their future, I moved on and hoped that other leaders would do better.

Working so hard on survival made me tired. I lost any sense of how to measure the fruits of my ministry. By the measures of longevity, market share, and customer satisfaction, I and my churches were failures, peddling a product that fewer and fewer people wanted and failing to make the bottom line year after year. I resented the generations that had gone before and had failed to prepare for our fast-changing times. I grew impatient with my elders' bewilderment at the failure of time-tested approaches to produce results. I could see the joy I had brought to ministry ebbing away. I was all spent out on death avoidance.

Looking death in the face has made me a better pastor. Shucking off the burden of steering my congregations away from death has helped me to see possibility. Letting go of the idea that there is salvation for the institution—and that it is my job to help the institution find that salvation—is tremendously freeing. It allows me to be bold and to encourage my congregation to be bold. No longer looking for reasons why things aren't working, I am free to pay attention to God, who I find busy as always making all things new.

I have begun to question the presumption that the survival of our church institutions is even what God wants, much less what God promises. Might it be idolatrous to assume that church as we know it is the future that God intends? Might we have built little towers of Babel and gotten lost in the beauty and everlastingness of the things we have built? Might it be God who is calling us toward death, even pushing us, because God wants so much to include us in the resurrection?

I find creative freedom and renewed faith in accepting that my church is a part of a great wave of dying. That acceptance enables me to let go of trying to do God's job and take up my own: pastoring a dying church through a faithful death and into whatever lies beyond. I want that freedom for you. I have seen too many churches beaten down for not thriving in this new era, seen too many try formula after formula and go nowhere. I have heard too many people blame each other, and their clergy and their children and their parents, for something that is larger than any one of us, larger than any one congregation or denomination. Too many congregations have been taught to believe that our own survival and high customer satisfaction ratings are the measure of our existence. Those are death-dealing reasons to exist. Living for our own survival pulls us under, sucks the joy out of whatever years we have left.

I have read plenty of elaborate analyses of how we got here, and why, and what is going on with the church. I am less interested in "Why?" than I am in "Now what?" I am a pastor now with maybe another two or three decades of ministry ahead if I am lucky enough to live long and prosper. I want to know how to care for God's people and be faithful to God now and into the immediate future. Death will come for me too. Until then, I want to make the most of my time on the road. For better or for worse, I have been called to ministry in an era of dying church.

This is a book of practices for faithful dying, for discovering resurrection where it is already popping up, for remembering that God is always doing a new thing, for finding beauty in the present, in one another and the neighbors God has given us, for loving and being loved, forgiving and being forgiven, for giving up on being church-builders and entrepreneurs and being people of the Way once again. These practices will help you to grieve and to live, and to rediscover why your church exists to begin with. These are the practices that have become my touchstones: the new measures of my ministry and the bedrock from which I pastor. This is a book of practices because it is easier to talk about faithful dying than it is to do it, because following Jesus is hard, and we all need more practice. Practicing our faith leads us closer to God and one another, and that is where we need to be.

The book is organized into three sections of three practices each, titled "Get Up," "Go Forth" and "A New Country." If you don't know where to start, try the beginning. If you're already deep into dying and rising and trying new things, feel free to grab hold of whatever makes the most sense to you. Each practice stands in relation to the others, but each chapter or section can also be taken alone. Some things will make more sense in your context than others. I hope and trust that some parts of my stories may trigger your imagination, may send you off dreaming and envisioning. We are meant to be dreamers and casters of visions. God wants that for us. The prophet Joel, with his echo in the book of Acts, identifies dreams and visions and prophecy as signs of the outpoured Spirit:

> "'In the last days it will be, God declares, that I will pour out my Spirit upon all flesh, and your sons and your daughters shall prophesy, and your young men shall see visions, and your old men shall dream dreams. Even upon my slaves, both men and women, in those days I will pour out my Spirit; and they shall prophesy.'" (Acts 2:17–18)

All of the practices in this book are about loving God and loving our neighbor, because those are the two things that we have been given to do. The beauty of those two commands is that just about anyone can do them in some way, at any stage of life and in any physical or mental condition. Any church can do them too, whether you are in a promising neighborhood or a dying community, whether your building is already on the auction block or you have years left to live. We are promised a share in the reign of God. Love is the way we claim that share. If we die in the midst of the work of love, we have nothing to fear but resurrection.

Resurrection is a funny thing. Jesus comes back, and no one recognizes him right away. He walks with them, and talks with them, and meets them in the garden. And all they see is a stranger.

Every time. In the garden, on the road to Emmaus, from the deck of a fishing boat, in the upper room. Outside the tomb.

Resurrection, it seems, is fundamentally different from revival or resuscitation. It does not produce the familiar, the immediately recognizable. It takes death into account and honors the gone-ness of that which went before. It is both the same and not the same. The sameness comes in the sacred, in the breaking of bread. The sameness reveals the holy link between old and new. Resurrection brings the discovery that what we thought was most important and most recognizable in that which is gone was, in fact, not it at all. In the breaking of the bread, in the cooking of breakfast, in showing one another our wounds, in a word spoken to the beloved, we discover what was essential and of God and un-killable in the one who has died.

We cannot expect that resurrection in our churches will be any less frightening or any less hard to recognize or any less shockingly new than the resurrection that lies at the center of our faith. We cannot claim resurrection as something that we are able to accomplish or call forth on our own timeline. Resurrection is not the fruit of our hard work or our outstanding vision or our determined creativity. Church growth is all about revival and resuscitation. Revitalization of that which has become moribund may be a fine goal in some cases. It is not the same as resurrection. Offering ourselves and our churches for resurrection means embracing a sure and certain death. We will not be as we are now, not once God is finished with us. We will not look or feel or smell the same, and yet that which was always holy about us will be holy still, revealed in new ways.

Because churches are not actually people, but rather made of people as well as buildings and gardens and giant coffee pots and rooms full of old stuff, death and resurrection may not be as clear-cut as they were in the life of Jesus. The people of your congregation will die one at a time, for the most part, not all at once. The roof will spring one leak at a time, and the floor in the hallway will peel away from the foundation gradually. Resurrection may begin to pop up while death is still taking place. The two may do battle. Maybe it isn't so different from our human lives.

A thousand small deaths and leaks and cracks—and a thousand small resurrections and little green plants springing up through broken concrete—all conspiring to prepare us for the big end and new beginning that will come for us all.

Resurrection is no easy way to new life. It tosses out our comfortable hopes for the familiar and rewrites the future in spite of us. Resurrection is God's alone. Our part in it is the dying part. The rising is all God's, and the shape of the Risen One belongs to God as well.

Section One

Get Up!

I hear a lot about churches feeling stuck. Most churches want to survive and have even tried some things to move themselves in that direction. Some have tried many, many things.

The real reason churches get stuck is not that they run out of ideas or that there aren't new ideas out there that they could grab hold of. The problem is that ideas don't save us. Only God can do that. And God's way leads through the cross, not around it or away from it.

The real reason churches get stuck is that we run up against the reality of death. The more ideas we try, the closer we get to the truth, which is that the next road we must take leads to death. After a while, all roads seem to lead in that direction, and it just gets too scary to go farther along any available path. Many churches have even tried going backwards. They find the way closed or simply discover another road that leads in the same direction.

So we do our best to stand still. Stuck. Churches can stay stuck for a remarkably long time. Our little congregations are often not as fragile as they look. But eventually the money runs out, the building falls down on us, or we just run out of the energy it takes to stand still in a fast-moving world.

In the Gospels, no one better exemplifies the temptation to stand still than Peter. When Peter, James, and John are on the mountaintop with Jesus, things get pretty awesome for a while. Moses and Elijah are there, and Peter sees this as a party that should go on and on. In the midst of his party planning, of course, we get the transfiguration: Jesus starts glowing; God starts speaking —awesome and terrifying, but still definitely awesome.

Then Jesus stops glowing, goes back to as close to normal as Jesus ever gets, sets his sights on the bottom of the mountain, tells the disciples that the party never happened, and heads toward Jerusalem.

To Peter, Jerusalem seems terrifying and not at all awesome. Jerusalem is the sort of place where even a genuine Messiah could get him or herself crucified. Jesus has confirmed that, yes, Jerusalem to the death is next on the agenda. When Peter wonders aloud if there might not be a better plan, Jesus says, "Get behind me, Satan."

Jesus, as far as we know, hasn't seen Satan since his stay in the desert way back at the beginning of his ministry. But he knows a well-crafted temptation when he sees one. Not going forward when we know that the road leads to death is a tantalizing temptation indeed. If even Jesus recognized it as tempting, who are we to sidestep Satan's wiles?

So don't feel bad about being stuck—but don't stay there, either. Start getting unstuck, and see what happens. Remember, the worst thing we have ahead is death, and that is coming for us anyway. If we don't insist on a whole strategic plan that takes us all the way to a full and solvent church forever, we can try taking one step and see where it leads.

The story of Abraham in Genesis starts with a curious phrase: Lech-l'cha. It's a command, and those Hebrew "ch"s have a hard, guttural sound that packs a nice punch. The literal meaning is something along the lines of "Walk-walk for yourself," idiomatically rendered as "Get up and go forth," or something along those lines. When you hear God say, "Lech- l'cha!" or "Get up and go forth!" you are in for a serious adventure: at the very least it will entail leaving everything you have ever known, undertaking perilous travel, and seeing the impossible become possible.

Collateral damage may include the loss and replacement of your name and everything you thought you understood about yourself.

When we consider the implications of Lech-l'cha, it is no wonder that many of us succumb to the temptation to sit back down. So instead of taking it all in one gulp, let's try just Lech: walk, or get up. The practices in this section will get you moving, literally and spiritually. They will get you unstuck and on the road.

Chapter One

Make Room

Where will the future happen in your church? If God is doing a new thing, where will God do it? Is there room? If those new people you have been waiting and praying for all these years show up tomorrow, full of energy and ideas for ministry, where will you put them? Are there rooms for them to meet in and practice their faith? Places for them to store their stuff? Are there extra keys to the kitchen?

In a church that isn't sure it has a future, making room for the future may seem like a strange way to start moving. It may even seem impossible. But making room for the future is a powerful act of faith. It assumes that there is a future, even if we can't see it. It assumes that God is not finished. And, unlike many more complicated practices, making room for the future is something that any church can get started on right away.

The dying church tends to fear the future. Who doesn't fear death, especially when we can feel it coming for us? We also resent the future, mistrust it. We suspect—correctly—that it will not belong to us. Occasionally, when given the opportunity to offer suggestions for how to approach the future, someone at St. Mary's will offer a variation on the anonymous comment: "Do whatever you want. I'll be dead soon anyway." Damn the future. It doesn't claim us; why should we invest even one more drop of energy or money in its selfish existence?

Jesus sums up the Way to God in two commandments: love God and love neighbors. On first impression, most of us find God much easier to love than those pesky neighbors with their annoying habits and sloppy ways. But loving God may be the far greater challenge. Neighbors irritate us, but they do it mostly in small ways. Their power over us is limited, just as is our power over them. God is lovable in our projections—fatherly in the best way, Jesus-y in a lamb-like, pastel sort of way, friendly to our desires, a good listener, and a good protector. But beyond our projections and Sunday school posters, God is big. Too big to love easily.

Our conflicted relationship with the future reveals our struggle with God's dimensions. The future belongs to God and to God alone. Our attempts to shape and control the future fail, at least most of the time. The fruits of our forward-looking offerings of love and effort are unpredictable and hard to see at best. The future reveals our limitations in uncomfortable ways. The future becomes the sticking point in our love for God. We want to love the future only in the ways that it belongs to us or to those in whose lives we have a direct stake. In owning the future, though, God insists that our love must project into the unknown, far beyond our recognizable selves.

Loving the future isn't easy. Especially when we sense that death is nearing—in our own lives or in our beloved institutions—it may be tempting to reject the future, even mock it or resent it. The future seems indifferent to the value of our existence, to all that we have been and tried to be, even to the gifts that we have offered with all our hearts. But loving the future is one of the most important ways we love God. Loving the future testifies that God will not be finished, even when we are. Loving the future testifies that God is God and that we are us, that God knows things that we don't know and does things that we can't do. Loving the future sacrifices our ability to know things and our ability to shape things—two of the human treasures that we guard most closely.

The gap between the way our popular culture talks about love and the way the Bible talks about love adds further difficulty. Love in songs and movies is all about feeling, usually portrayed just as it begins to bloom. Biblical love is not primarily a feeling, certainly not something to be fallen into. Biblical love is about offering, about sacrifice, about a willingness to see that which is ours—even that which is us—disappear into something so large we are not able to comprehend it. Biblical love is about trusting that the other belongs to God as well. Biblical love is about hanging in there for an entire lifetime and beyond.

Love requires concrete practices: feeding, welcoming, clothing, visiting, forgiving. We will not learn to love the future by sitting around attempting to summon warmer feelings. In the end, this is good news. Warm feelings about the future are, and will continue to be, in short supply in the dying church. In the midst of the chill of indifference, the resentment, and even the hotly burning anger, we can start practicing love for the future. Loving the future is a way to love God, to whom the future and all things in it belong.

One of the most concrete things you can do to love the future is to make room for it.

Most historic churches double as giant storage facilities. Every drawer and closet is full. Much of what is used in the present has to wedge into cardboard banker boxes and plastic tubs under tables, because there is not really room for the present, much less the future.

When we are pressed by many things in the present and things appear to be falling apart rather rapidly, cleaning out unused space may seem like a waste of precious time. It matters. Storing things that have passed beyond uselessness is an outward and visible sign of our love affair with the past. Throwing things away is hard because it requires us to grieve. As we turn our gaze to the future, we have to reckon the losses, add up the sorrows, let go of the things that will not be used again.

When everything is stuffed to capacity, various things start to happen. One is that only people "in the know" know where anything is. If someone new wants to put something somewhere, there is nowhere but a paper bag or plastic tub out in the open to offer them. Things also start getting locked up, and every closet has a different key. There is a sense that the church is already full—even if the pews are empty—and that nothing new or further is expected.

I served in a church where a donated collection of Christmas crèches from around the world had its own room: the Crèche Room. Hundreds of neatly labeled shoeboxes detailed the national origin of each crèche and the number of figures included. My favorite was "origin unknown," labeled as containing Jesus, Mary, Joseph, and "one extra guy." New people who started to fill in the cracks at that church liked crèches too, and they offered some lovely examples from the places they came from. But they were assured that there were already plenty of crèches—a whole roomful, in fact. Until all of those had gone on display, in their proper rotation, there would be no need for more. The crèche room had to go.

There are reasons churches become storage facilities. Some of them are the same reasons it happens to your house. Families and congregations alike produce prodigious amounts of stuff: paperwork, finished projects, half-finished projects, projects that we always meant to start, broken items that seem like they may be able to be fixed, age-appropriate items for people and eras that have now gone on to other things. Sorting stuff rarely seems like the best use of time in the present, so stuff accumulates. The places that were meant to store things—closets, filing cabinets, basements—become so clogged with the past, there is no hope for the present. Gradually stuff begins to encroach on the spaces that were meant for daily living: the dining room table, the surface of the desk, the shelves at the back of the sanctuary, the kitchen counters, valuable first-floor meeting rooms.

At St. Mary's, we found check stubs going back to the year of my birth and full congregational sets of 1940 hymnals and 1928 prayer books. We filled a spectacularly large dumpster with broken and obsolete furniture and equipment. Our neighbors carried off many things that we could no longer use or fix but they could use or recycle. We pulled out crumpled props from long-forgotten plays. We are still sorting miles of possibly usable fabric and mountains of crumbling construction paper.

On one cleaning day, I drew the line at keeping a Sunday School curriculum based entirely on filmstrips. The objection? "Someone is going to want to use that some day. I'm sure we've got a filmstrip projector somewhere upstairs." I'm sure we do. Probably two. We also have people already in their thirties, including our associate priest, who don't know what filmstrips are.

The thought of firing up a filmstrip projector for the iPad generation seemed mostly laughable, until I remembered to listen for the painful questions behind the objections. How can things obtained with hard-earned resources be so fleeting in their value? It probably took three board meetings and a special fundraiser to select and purchase that curriculum. How can we just fill dumpster after dumpster in a world already choking on trash? What happened to the wisdom of previous generations who washed and dried and saved and reused even squares of cellophane and old margarine containers? Who are these children that don't come to church anymore and are way too cool for filmstrips?

Disposable culture is scary, and not only because of the garbage patch in the ocean. For many lifelong church members, the fear of throwing away accumulated stuff goes hand in hand with the fear of being discarded themselves. When they see the not-quite-vintage (and not-quite-working) portable organ that they raised money to buy in the 1970s in the "to go" pile, it seems perilously close to trashing the love they contributed to the church—the trashing of "their" eras in favor of the era of some generation that doesn't even seem to want or love the church at all. Throwing things away feels like a rejection of the values of a generation that knew genuine hardship and responded by conserving just about everything.

Cleaning happens in stages.

Some things have to go.

Broken things need to go in the trash or be given to people who want to fix or repurpose them. Old financial records have a defined shelf life. A few nostalgia copies of old prayer books and hymnals will do for memory's sake (and no, there aren't any churches out there that want the whole congregational set as a donation).

Some things need to move.

Old program files and membership records may be worth saving, but not in the filing cabinet in the church office while current year receipts sit in banker boxes on the floor. Christmas pageant scripts from the 1970s are fun to take a look at, and may be even more interesting in one hundred years, but they don't need to live amongst the Sunday School supplies for this week. As we clean at St. Mary's, we save some things that may not be worth saving forever. Not ready to part with them yet, we box and label and put them out of the way, leaving the next generation to decide their fate.

Some things need to be kept.

Treasures, of course, but also some things that are not so obviously treasures. Cleaning out the kitchen cabinets at St. Mary's, we came upon a whole shelf of used soy sauce bottles, the sort that you would find on a restaurant table. They had been neatly washed and put away. The question of what to do with them brought the whole workday to a standstill. Memories flooded back of chatty afternoons in the kitchen with the giant can of soy sauce and a funnel, filling bottles for special events. Do they sell those giant cans anymore? The places people remembered buying them are closed now, as are so many Japanese American businesses St. Mary's remembers. A practical voice remarked that they sell those exact bottles, really cheap and already filled with sauce, at the local warehouse store. A slightly panicked voice wondered when the last time we needed that many soy sauce bottles had been. Unspoken but palpable was the question of whether we would ever have occasion to serve that much Japanese food again.

We kept the soy sauce bottles. We probably won't keep them forever, but the decision to keep them allowed us to get back to work, a little further along in our grief for what has gone before.

The distinction between throwing out stuff and throwing out people needs to be voiced loudly, explicitly, and often. There is a genre of church-turnaround material that is nearly gleeful in its proclamation that those who are holding the church back will just have to get out of the way. People who resist change are demonized, their grief-driven behaviors mocked. It is worth remembering that people who resist change may be standing in your way, but it is not really possible to stand in God's way. Trusting God to work lovingly with each of our hearts of stone will go a long way toward opening up gracious space for all of us to inhabit.

I can't promise that no one will leave as your congregation turns its face toward death in the hope of resurrection. The congregations I have served have certainly lost people along the way, for reasons good and bad. Some of them I miss more than others. But I don't ever believe that we can put people in the "to go" pile or rejoice in the loss represented by the departure of even the angriest longtime church member. The people who resist change (usually quietly) at St. Mary's are the same people who built the church, who offered themselves, for whom it has been the most safe and stable place amidst life's turbulence. Were their efforts perfect? No. Did they do a particularly good job reading the needs of the future? No. Is the present generation of leadership likely doing much better? No. We all depend on God's grace to bring beauty and life out of our motley efforts. As you make room for the future, don't forget to save room for the people who are struggling with change and grieving the losses of the past, present, and future. The result will be a roomier place for all, a place that will someday have room for you.

Cleaning out closets and file cabinets is mostly boring but also sad. It reminds us of all that was and all that isn't any more. Shredding files closes the door on old projects. Names from the past stare up from membership forms; pictures of those gone on to their rest hide in dusty corners. Unfinished projects glare sternly from their hiding places, judging our failure to follow through.

Sunday school is a notorious accumulator of stuff. For dying churches, it is also an open wound. Looking back through old records begs the questions: Were there really three hundred children enrolled in Sunday school that year? Where *are* those kids? Where are their kids?

St. Mary's Sunday school overflowed the building, occasioning the construction of an entire new wing. The Sunday school had its own superintendent, a prominent position of congregational leadership. Older members think of the Sunday school as having been bustling just twenty years or so ago. A quick check with a lifelong member in her thirties reveals that she remembers often being the only kid in Sunday school. So maybe forty years ago? Still, back in the day, our Sunday school was the place to be. Now we lose families, one by one, because we can't hope to compete with the glitzy menu of children's programs offered by larger, more affluent, suburban churches.

Two things seem to me to be true about historic church Sunday schools. One, they were run with love and great effort and an awful lot of small containers of dry beans and cones of yarn and endless jars of glitter. Two, they educated an entire generation up and out of our churches. The exact generations that overflowed the classrooms are now the ones who are nowhere to be found in church. The glitter is still waiting for their children.

Sorting the Sunday school closets pushes us into the most painful sort of recognitions. The jars of salvaged popsicle sticks and packets of dried-out glue sticks remind us of fun that is no longer, or at least not nearly as big as it used to be. We are forced into the realization that all the fun and activity and effort didn't really seem to get us to where we wanted to go. The feelings are tough, but the truth is sturdy ground. Cleaning allows us to let go of dreams of recreating past glory and look toward the future for new ways to connect with our children and equip them for life on the Way in their own era.

In the midst of all the junk in your closets and storage rooms, there will be treasures. Old photos, beautifully handcrafted things, sad-sweet reminders of all the life and prayer and conflict and community that have been contained in the walls of the church. Stuff tells parts of your story—both the good parts and the painful parts.

St. Mary's has a phenomenal collection of pictures, going all the way back to the church's founding in 1907. There are pictures with great historical value and a lot of very ordinary shots of people having picnics, playing games, acting in Christmas pageants, cooking meals, raising money, having fun, modeling the latest fashions and hairstyles. They tell a story of a community institution, by turns deeply connected to and deeply disengaged from its neighborhood—a haven for generations, a place of hope, and a place of loss.

At St. Mary's, we have begun to display treasures and use them to tell stories. Our best effort so far began with a dusty trophy case. It is hard to describe how large this trophy case is. It stands sentinel in a main hallway and requires a full-sized ladder to access the upper reaches. It weighs more than the Titanic. Some of the trophies are antiques; many have lost all identifying details over the years. The most recent, until this year, dated to the early 1990s. Several hold evidence of annual tournaments, begun and abandoned. It was a giant monument to a once-young and once-active church now waiting to die. That is not the whole story of St. Mary's, but it sure was the story told by the trophy case.

For St. Mary's centennial celebration, a talented parishioner and historian put together a series of posters with photos and artifacts from various eras. Nearly a decade later, we cleared the middle of the trophy case and displayed three of the posters, which had spent most of their short lives stacked in a dusty archive room upstairs. We chose the two posters from the earliest years of the parish and one with images from the centennial celebration in 2007, attended by many members of the far-flung parish family. Now every time someone comes to the building for the first time, I find a way to steer them past the trophy case. It gives me a chance to tell part of the story of the church and the neighborhood. I have seen more than one neighborhood teenager pause, skateboard in hand, mesmerized by the sight of another era in a familiar place, another generation of immigrants and their American-born kids, a panorama both similar to and distant from the present. One of the posters includes a racist flyer circulated in the neighborhood in the 1920s, exhorting neighbors to block the effort to construct a "Japanese Church." The skateboarders recognize the anti-immigrant rhetoric and shake their heads. "Dang. That's cold." I have been surprised at their fascination with the photos. I see them discovering that their own lives are part of a longer neighborhood story that includes many chapters and some enduring themes.

Treasures get lost when our churches turn into storage facilities. Old check stubs and disintegrating art supplies are not treasures. The notebooks with handwritten lists in Japanese of the first members of the church are. The stubs and the notebooks should not be tossed in a closet together. One should be shredded or trashed, the other lovingly displayed or carefully preserved. The first step is to recognize the difference. Finding and rescuing treasures is one of the joys of cleaning.

Once you have started making room, it is worth avoiding some of the ways that you ended up stuffed to the gills to begin with. I have cleaned many a church room only to have it full again in a year, with equally weird and useless stuff. We live in a culture of accumulation and clutter, and keeping the environment uncluttered is an opportunity for church to offer a respite and an alternative way forward to people who are struggling with the same issues at home.

Churches are magnets for gifts of weird stuff. Most people don't want to throw away things that have been useful, things that seem in some theoretical way like they might still be useful. But after a certain point, they don't want them in their garages either. So they give them to churches. Clothes that are hopelessly out of style with maybe just a few small moth holes and that smell that comes from long-term storage. Televisions encased in three-hundred-pound cabinets made of real wood. And the couches. Oh, the couches. St. Mary's had no fewer than ten old couches, deployed in hallways and underutilized rooms. One was at least fifteen feet long. I had never seen a couch so long. No good can come from taking in old couches. Some things are finished. We can have many feelings about our disposable society and how many good family times were lived on that couch, but none of that will be made any better or less painful by giving the couch to your church or by accepting such a gift on your church's behalf.

Don't save stuff if you don't have a reasonably clear use in mind. Give it away, or if no one wants it, throw it away. "Just in case" has filled far too many church closets.

We keep things because we are afraid of empty space. Empty space tells the truth about the emptiness of so many of our hopes, the ends of so many of our stories. Empty space demands faith. I'll be the first to admit that it scares me a little to see empty rooms that have just been cleaned out. "OK, God," I say on a regular basis, "Here's the space. Now what?"

I heard a sermon recently that referenced the image of the Spirit hovering over nothingness at the beginning of time in the New International Version translation of Genesis 1:2.

> Now the earth was formless and empty, darkness was over the surface of the deep, and the Spirit of God was hovering over the waters.

This image of the hovering Spirit helps me offer up the empty space in the hope that it will give the Spirit some wiggle room to do her thing. Despite my anxieties, I have never had a space stay empty for long in a church in the middle of a neighborhood full of people. When there is no empty space to be had, surprisingly little can happen.

Cleaning is an act of preparation for resurrection. It states that we expect new things and new people to need to use this space. It looks death squarely in the face. Cleaning rescues treasures and mementos that tell our sacred stories; it separates the valued from the no-longer-useful. It gets us moving and announces to the hovering Spirit that we are ready.

Here are some things that have filled empty spaces at St. Mary's—but only after the congregation cleared out the space to let them in:

- One marching tuba and one bass drum
- Thirty-one outreach workers for Home-Based Head Start
- Membership meetings (100+ people) of a Korean-Latino alliance for the rights of immigrant workers

- Three brand new 2014 trophies awarded by the local Oaxacan basketball league
- Costumes for performing traditional Zapotec dance
- One hundred cans of spray paint used for painting murals

If we hadn't made room, where would the tuba and spray paint go?

Chapter Two

Map the Terrain

How could we sing the Lord's song in a foreign land?
—Psalm 137:4

Thus says the LORD of hosts, the God of Israel, to all the
exiles whom I have sent into exile from Jerusalem to Baby-
lon: Build houses and live in them; plant gardens and eat
what they produce. Take wives and have sons and daughters; take wives for your sons, and give your daughters in
marriage, that they may bear sons and daughters; multiply
there, and do not decrease. But seek the welfare of the city
where I have sent you into exile, and pray to the LORD on
its behalf, for in its welfare you will find your welfare.
—Jeremiah 29:4–7

Many of our churches have lost track of where we are. We get
tangled up in who we are, and what we are doing, and worse yet,
how we are doing. When we do peek out, it looks like a foreign land
out there. Like the exiles of Jeremiah's time, we are tempted to hunker
down and seek out ways to stay who we are, in spite of where we are.
But Jeremiah's prophecy rejects this approach. Don't hunker down,
he says; don't wait for conditions to become more favorable. Be where
you are. Be there fully. Be with the people who are there with you.

So where are you? Who is there with you? What are the neighbors up to? Too often we begin conversations about getting the

neighbors to church with only the foggiest idea of who they are. These conversations inevitably drift toward the question of real and perceived obstacles to the goal of getting them engaged in the project of helping us grow. This chapter invites you to take a giant step back and just look.

Look back. Look out. Look up.

Mapping requires careful observation of the terrain from a variety of angles. A complete map shows relationships, paths, changes, natural features, human-built features, and more. If you are to map the context of your church, you will need to look in more than one direction, consider from more than one angle. To guide your looking, I've divided the process into three parts: look back; look out; look up. They don't necessarily have to be taken in order.

You may notice that the one direction I have not invited you to look is "in." Most dying churches need no further encouragement to spend hours lamenting the present and speculating about solutions for the future. Take a break from looking in, and try some other directions.

Don't get ahead of yourself. If you find yourself plunging into strategic planning after one walk through the neighborhood, take a deep and cleansing breath (and stop, for God's sake). This looking process takes a little time, both to do and to process. Looking is a start, not a middle or an end. Assume that God has time for you to get your bearings, especially if it's been a long time since anyone in your church had a look around. Do not assume that everything you see will provide an answer to your problems. Do not assume that anything you see will provide an answer to your problems, especially if the answers you seek are solutions to the big problem of death. In church, as in life, death is not a problem any of us mortals will solve. On the flip side, don't be too quick to dismiss what you see as unhelpful or irrelevant to your mapping project. God has been known to make wonderful use of some awfully strange raw material.

Step One: Look Back.

Historic churches were built to be part of neighborhoods and communities. They were built for specific people who lived in a specific place at a specific time. Fifty or one hundred or three hundred years later, it is rare, if not impossible to find those same people doing those same things in that same place. Often the church is all that is left of the community that founded it, the only sign of that which went before in a neighborhood that has undergone multiple and multilayered transformations in the intervening years.

Neighborhood transformation is a messy business. Even as a mostly white neighborhood becomes Japanese American, becomes African American, or a middle class neighborhood becomes poor, or a poor neighborhood gentrifies, there are vestiges of the previous lives of the neighborhood tucked within the fabric. A market with a Japanese name in a mostly Latino neighborhood, older people who didn't follow their younger generations to the suburbs, working class families hanging on as the hipsters take over, elegant houses divided into a dozen cramped apartments.

Knowing for whom you were built, and what happened to those people and that neighborhood, is one important part of the mapping terrain. It helps to explain how you became who you are, why you do what you do, and what parts of who you are and what you do might or might not fit where you are now.

St. Mary's neighborhood began life as Uptown, an early suburb of downtown Los Angeles. Craftsman houses sprang up after the turn of the twentieth century. Japanese Americans and others fleeing the crowding of downtown settled there. St. Mary's moved there too, a few years after opening its doors as a mission downtown in 1907. By the 1930s, the neighborhood was settling in to itself, adding apartment buildings. St. Mary's replaced its original house-church with a "proper" building: large and elegant and very churchy.

World War II came, and with it came the internment of the Japanese American population of the West Coast. St. Mary's was the assembly point for Uptown families; a copy of the evacuation order still hangs in the back of the church. Archival photographs show church and neighborhood families, huddled on the front steps of the church, facing the unknown with the scant household possessions they were allowed to bring along.

After losing all of its Japanese inhabitants during the War, Uptown was never the same. Some Japanese families returned, especially those fortunate enough to have been able to hang on to property through the upheaval and aftermath of the war. But many of the Nisei (second-generation Japanese Americans), having spent their young adulthood in camp and in the U.S. military, joined the postwar exodus to the suburbs. St. Mary's became a place to come back to—not the neighborhood church—for many of its members. Uptown became "the old neighborhood," a center-city place in contrast to LA's sprawling postwar suburbs.

St. Mary's has a lot of documentation of the early years of Uptown, and there are plenty of people who can tell the neighborhood's story up to about 1950. After that, the story of the neighborhood becomes fuzzier. St. Mary's grew and thrived as a mostly commuter church. It still served a primarily Japanese American congregation, but others joined in—African Americans, Filipinos, Anglos, Belizeans, people of mixed heritage. At some point in the 1950s and '60s, a wave of Japanese Americans from Hawaii found its way to St. Mary's, strengthening the congregation and its Japanese heritage but also infusing new traditions and a new spin on the Japanese American experience. The Hawaii families lived far from the church without exception, but the Episcopal Church was still relatively segregated, and more than one family tells the story of visiting their neighborhood Episcopal Church only to receive subtle and not-so-subtle cues that they ought to check out St. Mary's. When they did check it out, they liked what they found: a warm community deeply steeped in Japanese American culture, a place for their children to grow up in a supportive environment, a place where there was space for the particular cultural mix that they brought from Hawaii, a refuge from a surrounding world that was still sometimes hostile to Japanese-ness.

Who lived in Uptown in the 1960s and '70s? No one who is there now seems to know in any detail. The current residents, mostly Latino and Korean, began arriving in large numbers in the 1980s. By then, St. Mary's focus had turned inward. Increasingly, its members stayed within the bounds of the church property, interacting with the neighborhood mostly through an annual bazaar-carnival. Even that event was a magnet for Japanese Americans and Episcopalians from outside the neighborhood, and local folks may have made up a minority of participants. Some reports indicate that the congregation considered a move to the growing Little Tokyo neighborhood on the east side of downtown sometime in the 1970s. A vision was hatched to attract new Japanese immigrants who began arriving to work in the auto industry in Southern California in the 1980s, but most of those new immigrants settled far from St. Mary's.

Somewhere along the way, Uptown became Koreatown, a center of Korean businesses with mostly Latino immigrant residents from Central America and Oaxaca (a state in southern Mexico, many of whose residents speak native languages in addition to Spanish and identify primarily by ethnicity—Zapotec, Mixtec, Mixe—rather than their national identity as Mexicans). The 1980s epidemic of urban violence swept the neighborhood, and many memories from that period carry gunshots as their soundtrack. The 1992 riots revealed deep fractures in the community, further frightening suburban St. Mary's members who saw news footage shot blocks from the church of burning buildings, looting, and armed shopkeepers.

The choices of the past continue to affect St. Mary's relationship with its neighbors. A few neighborhood residents bring warm memories of the bazaar-carnival, but many more speak of how closed the church seemed to the local community. Even people whose children attended preschool in St. Mary's parish hall reported that they weren't sure it was an active church. The church's fascinating history, including the fact that Koreatown had once been a Japanese American neighborhood, was a well-kept secret. Even St. Mary's architecture reflects a lack of priority on neighborhood outreach. The church is large, and occupies the better part of a city block, but it has few signs. The street address leads to a gate that is locked most of the time, and only those who already know where they are going are likely to find the parking lot. The building is painted a neutral color, without accents or eye-catching features. The street level stained glass windows are covered with protective plastic that has long since yellowed and turned opaque. It looks like a place where all the life is hidden on the inside.

Knowing something about the history of your community and the history of the church's relationship to its surroundings is key to understanding the present. The past has many ways of infiltrating the present. If nothing else, the past has led to the present in your congregation, and most of us are a few demographic and cultural shifts behind by now. Looking back will help you to look out with eyes to see.

As you look back, be clear-eyed but gentle. Don't shy away from the ways that your church has disengaged with its community, but be careful about judging the failings of the past too harshly. Hating the past will not help you love the future any better. Being honest about where you have been, on the other hand, will help with everything that happens from here on out.

Step Two: Look Out!

If you are only going to look in one direction, it should definitely be out. Having some sense of history helps to contextualize what you see and to factor shifting contours and changing landscapes into your map. But if you don't look out, all the other looking will come to naught.

By the time I got to St. Mary's in 2011, it had been years since most of the congregation had ventured beyond the bounds of the parking lot except to come and go by car from the surrounding network of Los Angeles's famous freeways. Even the annual bazaar-carnival had been mothballed as the core volunteers aged and grew tired. Stepping across the street to view the church and walking around the block was a new experience for nearly everyone on the vestry, or church board. Despite having done a lot of thinking and praying about St. Mary's future, even recommitting to making St. Mary's a neighborhood church, most St. Mary's members were unaware of recent changes in the neighborhood: the slowing of Latin American immigration, the growing Korean population, the gentrification driven by South Korean investment, the simmering tension between Latino and Korean neighbors.

At each of our leadership retreats since I began ministry with St. Mary's, we have gotten out into the neighborhood on foot. Heading out into our own neighborhood may seem like an odd way to retreat. Retreats are meant to pull us back from the everyday, to create new space, to quiet the noise of our lives so that God's voice is clearer to our ears. We could have gone away to a lovely spot by the beach, or borrowed the facilities of one of the generous and well-heeled parishes in our diocese that welcomes city vestries to get out of the urban chaos. But we really didn't need more time to reflect on what we already knew. We needed to get away from our own assumptions, to retreat from the entrenched ways of doing things that had become second nature, to step out of our own comfort. The place to do that was right around us at the church.

What Did We See?

Here is a sampling of the images that came back, the lessons we took from them, and the questions we asked, as we began to imagine the lives of our neighbors and how we might connect with them.

Quiet streets: The first year we were out bright and early on Saturday morning. The neighborhood was very sleepy. It made some people wonder if the hundreds of thousands of people were hiding from us. It made me wonder if everyone sleeps this well on Sunday mornings, too.

Gardens: Our neighbors are growing things, from front yards made of lettuce to magical hanging squash gardens strung through the trees. Most people have little outdoor space to call their own, but the year we took photographs on our walk, every group came back with pictures of gardens.

Places of prayer: A dried palm cross tucked in a garage window remains one of my favorite photos. Our neighbors are praying. Little shrines and small holy objects are tucked here and there with signs of recent use.

The informal economy at work: While much of the neighborhood is sleepy in the morning, 8th Street—a couple blocks from the church—is hopping. Shopping carts with propane tanks attached for cooking, coolers full of steaming tamales, setups to squeeze fresh orange juice, and pop-up yard sales all attest to the creativity of our neighbors and how they survive on the economic margins.

A whole lot of Korean: The conventional wisdom at St. Mary's when I arrived was something that had been closer to true in the past: Koreatown was a Korean business district, but few Koreans actually lived there. A close inspection of several of the many strip malls labeled only in Korean revealed businesses that clearly cater to the daily needs of a local population. Unlike Little Tokyo, where the Japanese American presence is largely commercial and cultural, Koreatown is home to many Koreans. This was a new reality to absorb as St. Mary's assessed its neighbor situation.

Graffiti: I live in Koreatown, about a mile from the church. When my oldest child was two or three, she learned the word for graffiti. It delighted her. Finally something that was absolutely everywhere, that she could point out. "There's a graffiti! Another one! Look mommy, a graffiti!" I remember feeling my heart sink, the grit of our urban setting encroaching on the romance of raising cosmopolitan city children. The area around St. Mary's has even more graffiti than where I live. There's graffiti on the palm trees and on the abandoned couches. Most of it represents MS-13, the active gang that claims us as part of its territory.

Thriving spaces in our neighborhood: After a retreat that in part involved struggling with the difficult questions of our church's future, we packed into a huge, noisy, crowded restaurant a block from the church, barely managing to get a table, even with a reservation. People are out there. Our neighborhood—at the right times of day, and in the right places—is vibrant. This was a little painful to realize, given how quiet our church was most Sunday mornings at that time.

Stuff we know nothing about: One year we stumbled onto a Korean community fun run and fundraiser. All the printed information was exclusively in Korean, with only cryptic bits of English translation, even on the sponsoring organization's website.

While I'm sure we could have found things out with a little dedicated research, this encounter brought home to us the ways in which we are isolated from the Korean community around us by language and culture, an impression that has been reinforced by nearly every attempt we have made to connect with that part of our neighborhood.

On a lighter note, one of the things we found our Korean neighbors doing at their fundraising event was a dance that everyone seemed to know, involving motions that looked like riding a hobby horse. I was the only one on the retreat who recognized "Gangnam Style," but a month or two later, when the quirky K-pop song hit the U.S. mainstream, St. Mary's board members were ahead of the cultural curve.

Banana trees: I came back with dozens of pictures of banana trees, something people still occasionally tease me about. I started with a nice one that just seemed photogenic. Then I noticed that they were everywhere. Tucked into small spaces in front of and beside apartment buildings, in the yards of houses, even in the median strips.

The funny thing about the proliferation of banana trees in Los Angeles is that LA's climate is all wrong for growing bananas. It's too dry and too cold. Most of these trees produce nothing but beautiful green leaves. When a bunch of bananas does grow, it usually stays green and tiny. Whatever our neighbors are doing, they are not growing bananas.

The banana trees were my contribution, so I came back with a theory—two theories really. One is that people use the leaves for steaming things like tamales and meat. My other theory has to do with home. If home is filled with banana trees—as it is for so many of our immigrant neighbors—what better way to make a new home than take what the neighborhood hands you . . . and add banana trees.

Our Church:

Last but not least, we saw our church from the other side of the street, as our neighbors see it.

We saw large blank walls, and virtually no signs visible from the street. We saw that, despite its size, St. Mary's melts into its surroundings, nearly invisible at the heart of its block. I told people what I had heard again and again from neighbors: "I didn't know it was a church." What had seemed ludicrous from inside the traditional sanctuary became believable from across the street.

Every time we get out there, more is revealed about who is around, who is at the table, who isn't, who eats what, who eats together, and who won't eat with who else. Every year we are different too. We are more sophisticated in our discernment of detail. Where the first year, most vestry members might have seen Latinos, they now wonder if they are Mexicans or Guatemalans. Salvadorans? People from the Mexican state of Oaxaca? Oaxacans from the mountains or the valley? These distinctions have meaning because we know more people, have asked more questions, and have some context for understanding what we see.

Step Three: Look (Things) Up

The Internet age offers vast quantities of information about just about anything. That certainly includes your neighborhood. When you have questions, one approach is to look things up. While looking up information about your surroundings is no substitute for experiencing those surroundings firsthand, it can provide a helpful complement to your direct observations.

During the rector search that led to my call to serve as their priest, St. Mary's obediently looked at the demographic reports that have been all the rage in the dying church in recent years. The following line stood out for me when I read the parish profile.

"Within a three-mile radius of St. Mary's, there are roughly 693,000 people."

That one sentence contains the entire universe of poignancy, insanity, tragedy, and possibility that is the life and death of the historic church. Seven hundred thousand people! With that many people around, what kind of pathetic failure of a church isn't growing? Seven hundred thousand people? How in the heck does a motley group of 50 to 100 Sunday commuters get to know 700,000 people? What would 700,000 people do to a little church if they did come?

Unpacking the 700,000 became one of the mantras of my ministry. Seven hundred thousand is a whole lot of people in a three-mile radius. Ours is a land of two- and three-story buildings. One thing we know about our neighbors is that they are squished together rather tightly.

One key to working with demographic information is finding the right radius. The program that our denomination offers generates a report based on a three-mile radius. In our context, three miles seemed tiny to commuters, some of whom drive thirty miles to get to church. Those of us who actually live in our dense urban area helped the commuters to understand that three miles is actually way too big. Within that three-mile radius are several distinct neighborhoods between which there is very little mixing. The residents of the 1920s mansions built for early movie stars and producers in Hancock Park rarely stray into Koreatown. The poorer and more crowded Pico Union and MacArthur Park-Westlake districts are filled with large families without cars for whom even bus fare is a stretch.

The area we settled on to study was roughly one mile square, bounded by major streets. We were able to explore this area using HealthyCity.org, a free website that uses mostly census data. It didn't give us the churchy information that the denominational report did, but it painted quite a vivid picture of the material lives of our neighbors—quite a different picture than that painted by the three-mile radius.

Here are the highlights: Our one-mile square neighborhood is about 65 percent Latino. Half of those people are of Mexican ancestry, the other half mostly Central American. Another 30 percent are Asian, mostly Korean. Ninety percent of our neighbors live on less than $50,000 in annual household income; a staggering 50 percent on less than $25,000. Ninety-five percent are renters. An *LA Times* article identifies our zip code as having the second-most crowded housing in the nation. Another *LA Times* article asserts that as many as one-third of adults in our area lack immigration status in the U.S. As I read those statistics, I lost my last shred of illusion that St. Mary's has long to live as a middle class church.

Demographics can't give you a plan. They won't solve your problems. The church is not dying primarily from a lack of statistical information. But demographics will burst some of your bubbles. They will awaken questions and whisperings of possibility that deserve further exploration. They will help to tell you which of the many purportedly helpful pieces of advice coming from outside your congregation are likely to be at all applicable in your context. Just to give one example, the conventional wisdom that it takes an average Sunday attendance of around one hundred to support a full-time priest or minister only works if families pledge more than $1,000/year on average. When the median family in your neighborhood is looking up at the poverty line, this is not a realistic expectation. Approaches that fit homogeneous areas will be different from the ones that work best in diverse communities.

Looking up basic information is a start. It gets you moving on your mapping project. Once you've got some basics and are starting to draw your map, you can move into the realm of pilgrimage to enter more deeply into the lives and stories of your neighbors.

A Little Note

If your congregation doesn't share St. Mary's clear sense of ethnic identity and history, you may wonder how some of this story of heritage and change relates to your context. If your church started its life serving a predominantly or exclusively white community, it may not think of its history in the ethnically defined terms that St. Mary's does. Anglo or white American identity is the norm by which all other ethnic American experiences tend to be measured. Be assured, however, that any non-Anglo neighbors you have now will likely perceive your historically white church as ethnically specific—in other words, not for them. Your ministry will need to embrace this reality rather than running from it and take it into account as you seek engagement with your neighbors.

Chapter Three

Turn Out Your Pockets

Abundance is a trendy word in church-speak these days. In just the last few days, I have been asked to give out of my abundance, invited to live out of my abundance, and admonished to recognize my abundance. For dying churches, reality is about scarcity. We recognize ourselves as dying because there is not enough of something we need to keep going—usually people, energy, money, or building resources. Sometimes all of the above. We see ourselves coming up short, and we know that we must either change course or our course will be cut short for us. Scarcity is real in our world; many of our neighbors and communities live without the essential things they need as well. We diminish ourselves less than we think we do by acknowledging that all is not abundant in our corner of the world. By standards of growth and success we may come up short, but we share the daily bread of our neighbors' lives in a new way when our resources dwindle.

In a reality of scarcity, it is easy for dying congregations to feel like we have little or nothing left to offer. We look at other churches that seem more popular and successful, and we count the ways that they are able to meet the needs and desires of the communities they serve. We also tend to hang on tighter and tighter to what we have left—to the things that stand between us and the end of church as we know it.

Imagine yourself among the disciples. Jesus has been preaching and healing all day. Your job is mostly crowd control. It's hot and dusty, and there are a lot of people. A *lot* of people. Kids, elders, parents, people who look like they should not be out in the sun. People who are not getting along with each other, who don't know how to wait in line patiently.

You are tired and ready to go home. Jesus' energy seems inexhaustible, but you know that he too must be worn down by the day, weighed down by grief over the news he has just received of John the Baptist's murder. Surely he too needs a break.

You consult with the other disciples. Everyone agrees. It is time to put an end to this endless day. You are chosen to approach Jesus. "Jesus," you say, once you have his attention, "It's getting late. This is a lonely place and all these people need to eat. It seems like time to send them off so that they can buy food in the surrounding towns."

Now all day long, the one thing that has kept you going is knowing that eventually things will settle down. Eventually you will get to sit down, and when you do, there is a small sandwich in your tunic pocket, and you will sit, and you will eat it, and you will relax for a few minutes. As the day wears on, the bliss of that sandwich and the eating moment loom larger and larger in your consciousness. That is going to be a good sandwich. The ground will be warm beneath you. You will take off your sandals and wiggle your toes. You will stretch your legs. You will bite in and taste the bread and salted fish, and the world will be good to you.

Jesus looks at you and says, "You feed them. Give them something to eat." You protest that this is clearly impossible. Too many people. Way too many people. Do you know what it would cost to buy the most minimal meal for all these people? Where would you find that kind of quantity for sale? How would you get it here? And the distribution . . . can you imagine getting these people to wait in line?

Jesus looks at you and smiles a little slyly. "Is that a sandwich in your pocket?"

Your sandwich, your poor little sandwich, just some bread and fish, and the only thing in the world you are really looking forward to right now. Jesus wants it. He wants it for all these people when it won't possibly be enough, and the only result will be that you don't get your moment. No sandwich, no sitting down, no sandals off, no stretchy toes. Your sandwich will be gone before you know it, everyone will still be hungry, and the day will be a total loss.

You seriously think about turning and leaving, heading out of town, just you and your sandwich. But it's Jesus. So you give him the sandwich. Your friends follow, giving up the small treats they have in their own pockets. Jesus takes them, and blesses them, and breaks them, and gives them back to you, and you are still on your feet, but you are feeding people, one after another, and more and more, and even you get to eat some, and it starts to seem like more than what you brought, and you have forgotten all about stretching your toes, because something is *happening*. Jesus has done something. He has done it with your sandwich.

But first you had to give it up.

Our era is full of churches that are dying, grieving, bewildered at how much they have already lost. Many share a recent experience of pouring out resources in hope of a turnaround and receiving little reward in return. Some have slowly, gradually given up almost everything—all the space is rented out, the bank accounts are tapped from filling growing deficits. Even our dignity may be left in shreds along the way as we try things that are not authentic to who we are in the hopes of being relevant and contemporary. It's no wonder that we hang on tightly to what is left. When we feel like we have failed, it's easy to lose sight of the potential of what is left. It feels like it is too little too late.

It is time to see what we have in our pockets. Jesus sees it anyway; you know he does. "You can't take it with you" applies to churches just like it applies to people. It is time to give it all up to God's purpose and see what your meager resources can do. It is time to let go of whatever small morsel you had been saving and with it your well-earned rest and your last hope of a comfortable end to the day. Turn the pockets inside out, and leave them hanging there awhile, just so everyone can see that you are all in. Risk the joy of seeing what wasn't enough for you become more than enough for Jesus.

When I teach kids about church, I like to turn them loose in the sanctuary, letting them look closely and touch the holy things. They always have a lot of questions. One little girl examined the offering plate in detail, poking insistently at the bottom and around the edges: "This is where we put the money for God, right?" Right. "So how do you get it to God?" She was looking for the secret trap door.

Everything in your church pockets was purportedly given for the glory of God. Our fundraising pitches and stewardship drives all frame giving to the church as a way of giving to God. By that logic this is all God's stuff anyway. *We* have to become the secret trap door in the offering plate: the way the money and the stuff get to God.

St. Mary's has some land—a rare commodity in the center of the city. Foresightful church members bought up property around the church back when it was a little more affordable. They formed an organization to hold the property for the benefit of the church. It was meant to be room for the future as it unfolded, envisioned at a time when the church was booming. Various visions have come and gone. My office contains a whole closet of blueprints for proposed church expansions, both built and left unbuilt. At one time, the priest imagined a retirement home for aging Japanese Americans. Another facility built for that purpose largely supplanted that need. A group of younger members put together a plan for transitional housing for battered women and their children. Older members of the congregation had their doubts about committing the property for that use. Eventually the plan was scrapped, leaving a bitter taste of intergenerational conflict. The three lots with aging houses on them produced small amounts of rental income for years. When a new generation took over leadership of the organization, they evaluated the condition of the houses and decided that their time as landlords was coming to an end. By the time I arrived, two of the houses had been torn down, and the third was scheduled for demolition. Tenants had been relocated, and weeds were growing rapidly. The church was left with infrastructure for an imagined future that never came.

The extra land was an obvious and important piece of what St. Mary's held in its pockets—valuable, but unsightly and burdensome in its current state. The land was a nest egg of sorts, both a hedge against an uncertain future and a painful reminder of dreams of endlessly expanding possibility. By 2011, the most often talked about use for the vacant lots was creating additional parking. St. Mary's has a pretty good-sized parking lot by urban LA standards, but it doesn't hold as many cars as the church does people. A few times a year, the church hosts a large event—usually a funeral—that fills every last seat. Cars wander the congested blocks around the church, looking for spots. As most of our members drive in from parking-rich suburbs to come to church, our pretty-good city parking lot looks less than adequate.

On the face of it, creating more parking for big funerals seemed to me like maybe the most depressing possible use for vacant church-owned land. I had to take several deep breaths, step back, and be at St. Mary's for a little while before I could begin to understand the weight of the land-use question.

St. Mary's has done a lot of funerals in recent years, although one sign of the shrinking congregation is that I have not done nearly as many funerals per year as my immediate predecessors. There are fewer people left to die. Being a church that does more funerals than weddings or baptisms is supposed to be one of those marks of shame that makes the dying church hang its head and concede defeat. But St. Mary's does funerals well. It does them with a quiet dignity, and it does them with pride. Funerals at St. Mary's are acts of hospitality, acts of honor, service to a community that is saying goodbye to a significant generation in its history. They are, in a sense, the ministry of the church at its best.

Most of the funerals at St. Mary's in the past decade or so have been for members of the Nisei generation, the U.S.-born children of the Japanese immigrants who arrived in the United States in the first decades of the last century. They are the generation that built St. Mary's, transforming it from humble mission to proud parish, from immigrant outreach to American church. They are the generation that spent their youth in the shadow of the Second World War—from internment camps in American swamps and deserts to the battlefields of Europe and the Pacific. They found themselves transformed into enemy-citizens whose own country turned against them, requiring them to prove and perform their loyalty.

There is never anything ordinary about marking the end of an individual life. But there is something more than the individual that is laid to rest at a Nisei funeral at St. Mary's. The mourners—whether Nisei themselves, their third- and fourth-generation descendants, or even their neighbors and friends from beyond the Japanese American community—feel the weight of this passing generation, the loss of history that remains unhealed. This generation and its experiences has come to define much of what it means to be Japanese American, and yet the ones who can tell the stories firsthand are slipping away, one by one.

St. Mary's offers the best of its hospitality to the dying Nisei through dignified worship and fellowship: the telling of stories, beautiful food and flowers, and yes—parking, especially for our elders, for whom the trip from car to building is more slow and painstaking with each passing year. Funerals are a homecoming time, a sign of the role St. Mary's has played in Los Angeles' Japanese American community for more than one hundred years. People may no longer live in the neighborhood. Fewer and fewer of them may make the drive to worship in our sanctuary each Sunday. Most of their children and grandchildren have long since built full lives in the suburbs. But people come home to be buried. Funerals are St. Mary's chance to be home again.

Until I lived a few of these funerals and glimpsed their significance, I could not begin to play a helpful role in the conversation about land. We have not ended up paving over the vacant lots for parking. But putting parking into its proper context—as one small piece of a much larger grief—is essential as we move forward. Being asked to give up the dream of proper parking is more than just giving up a dream of paving over dirt. It is a piece of our sandwich.

Even as the grief for lost future possibilities continues to run its course, St. Mary's has started offering our land. We began by talking about short- to medium-term uses for the land—things that might not mean giving up all potential future uses. We started showing the land to anyone who was around, and mentioning that we were thinking about using it for something worthwhile. We stood around with our pockets turned out.

Opportunities began to arrive almost immediately. A well-funded collaboration of community groups working to stem childhood obesity wanted to build a garden for local families with small children. A group that delivers meals to people with AIDS and other serious illnesses wanted to grow organic vegetables. All of a sudden people were showing up, offering resources that would make our land feed God's people. It helped that St. Mary's had already turned one small piece of backup-parking land into a community garden. It helped that one of the key players in the new garden collaboration was himself Japanese American and was able to present the vision in a way that honored St. Mary's history and heritage. It helped that growing things is such an important part of the history of the Japanese American community in LA. Many of St. Mary's members could see the transformative value of a garden.

We have two community gardens now, one on either side of the church. A third garden grew thousands of pounds of food for people and their families impacted by the crisis of serious illness. It is now the new campus for the Head Start preschool that had—for nearly two decades—shared "temporary" space in St. Mary's parish hall, setting up and breaking down portable classrooms every week to make room for Sunday church activities. Because we had begun the process of offering the land and seeing its beauty as a part of God's project, we were ready to give it over to this much longer-term use when the opportunity presented itself.

The process of offering up the land has been transformative. The board of three members of ancestral St. Mary's families who are the current stewards of the land-holding organization have had the closest view. They can be goofy—easy jokers who insist that their true desire for the land is to build a go-kart track for

their personal use. They are also practical, multitalented profes-
sionals who know how to negotiate contracts *and* set fence posts.
They are not given to a lot of frilly talk about God's providence.
But looking back over the last few years and the possibilities that
have opened up and the way that the land is becoming a gift to
the community and a ministry for the church leaves even them
shaking their heads in something like awe.

St. Mary's is not finished turning out pockets. The preschool
move opened up the parish hall to many more activities: exercise,
cooking classes, homework space, dance, drumming. Now that
we don't have to keep doors locked for security, we also have
the possibility of keeping the sanctuary open for prayer during
the day. Each of these offerings requires its own adjustments and
sacrifices. We will have to trust both God and our neighbors to
care for places and things that have been built and preserved with
love. I recognize that it is easier for me to call on people to place
that trust because I have not been along for all the sacrifices that
went into building St. Mary's. I have not lived its full meaning as
a refuge for a community under siege.

Turning out pockets means finding more and more things that
we might be called to give. Each time we see our gifts received
and multiplied, we have a little more courage to offer something
else we may have been holding back. The temptation to keep the
pockets sealed never really goes away, but we begin to see that we
have more to offer than we would have thought, and to find the
joy in the offering.

What is still in your pockets? What feels like it might be too
much to offer? What hopes do you hold for a peaceful end to the
day? What are you keeping in reserve? What feels like it might
not be enough to do much with anyway? Who in your community might have better ideas than you do about what to do with
your space or your money, if they knew it was available for God's
purposes?

Jesus asks for all we have and says, "You feed them."

Section Two

Go!

You've gotten up. You've made some room. You've taken a look outside. You've turned out your pockets. It's time to go. If you sit back down now, none of that good and faithful practice—not to mention hard work—will do much good. It's time to engage with these neighbors you've discovered: to enter their worlds on their terms as best you can; to try doing some things with the materials at hand; to risk saying yes to the people who come your way, even if you're not at all sure they are the ones you were waiting for.

Our beloved Bible is a book of people on the move. Abraham gets up and goes. Moses leads the people out of Egypt and into the wilderness. They eventually get to the promised land, but they don't get to stay there forever. They go into exile. They come back. Jesus heads into the wilderness, comes back, and spends his whole public ministry on the go, traveling from Galilee to Judea, up the mountain, back down the mountain, on to Jerusalem. He walks the road to the cross. He gets up and walks out of the tomb. He meets his disciples on the road to Emmaus. Paul is struck down on the road to Damascus. He hits the road again almost immediately, traveling the empire, preaching and teaching and founding Christian communities. Before we were Christians, we were the people of the Way, people on the move.

The gospel is a path, not a place: something dynamic, ever in motion and in practice.

So go. Now is the time not to let the grass grow under your feet, to get a little dirt under your nails. Now is the time to be bold.

Jesus shows us that in walking freely toward our own death, we discover the path to the only life worth living. He tells us again and again what the prophets told the people of Israel and what God told the prophets and leaders when God first called them: "Do not be afraid."

Do not be afraid to look stupid. Do not be afraid to leave your places of comfort. Do not be afraid not to know the answers. Do not be afraid of small messes. Don't even be afraid of big messes. Or be afraid. Be afraid, because human beings are basically scaredy-cats. But do all these things anyway, even though you are afraid. Ask good questions. Explore new territory. Put yourself out there. Give out keys. On the road to death, we have little to lose and everything to gain.

> Then Jesus told his disciples, "If any want to become my followers, let them deny themselves and take up their cross and follow me. For those who want to save their life will lose it, and those who lose their life for my sake will find it. For what will it profit them if they gain the whole world but forfeit their life? Or what will they give in return for their life?" (Matt. 16:24–26)

The three practices in this section will take you deeper into the life of your community. They will begin to put flesh on the bones that you discovered through the practices of the first section. They will begin to put your congregation on the map that you have made. They will get you out there, exploring the terrain, and they will not give you much time to worry about what you are going to do with all that space you have cleared out or who is going to want to eat your sandwich. After all, that is God's work. This section is all about our work.

"Make Pilgrimage" is about moving toward your neighbors in

a respectful and life-giving way rather than just waiting for them to move toward you. "Try Things" is about trying things . . . specifically, things that you aren't sure will work, or might make you look foolish, or might be outright catastrophes. "Say Yes" is about those miraculous moments when your neighbors actually come to you, and about recognizing those moments as gifts from God and making the most of the small openings that can lead to holy relationships.

For as long as we are here, church is meant to be about community. If we become just one more institution bent on meeting the bottom line and driven by customer satisfaction, we are dead already. This section is about entering into deeper relationship with the local community and surroundings: reimagining and rediscovering our value and our life as places of and in community.

Chapter Four

Make Pilgrimage

> Rejoice with those who rejoice, weep with those who weep.
>
> —Romans 12:15

Hopefully in the course of your observations you have caught some glimpses of your neighbors living their lives. You may even have some answers to the questions of what they do for fun, how they enjoy one another's company, what they celebrate. You may have seen evidence of the brokenness of your community. Observing from a safe distance is a key first step, especially if you, like many historic congregations, are starting from a place of disconnection. Now it's time to get more deeply into this business of being neighbors. If we are going to weep and rejoice together— rather than just watching one another—we had better start finding ways to share the ups and downs of our lives, to enter into one another's territory.

At no point in Jesus' ministry did he wait for people to come to him. Some did come, but only because they had already heard that Jesus was on the move in their communities, getting out there, meeting people, healing them, teaching things that made sense and changed lives. At no point did Jesus suggest that the disciples set up camp in one pretty building, create quality programs, put out a sign, design a website, and wait for people to arrive. He sent them out, from town to town.

> After this the Lord appointed seventy others and sent them on ahead of him in pairs to every town and place where he himself intended to go. He said to them, "The harvest is plentiful, but the laborers are few; therefore ask the Lord of the harvest to send out laborers into his harvest. Go on your way. See, I am sending you out like lambs into the midst of wolves. Carry no purse, no bag, no sandals; and greet no one on the road. Whatever house you enter, first say, 'Peace to this house!' And if anyone is there who shares in peace, your peace will rest on that person; but if not, it will return to you. Remain in the same house, eating and drinking whatever they provide, for the laborer deserves to be paid. Do not move about from house to house. Whenever you enter a town and its people welcome you, eat what is set before you; cure the sick who are there, and say to them, 'The kingdom of God has come near to you.'" (Luke 10:1–9)

Off the disciples went, to the places where people lived, to eat their food and partake of their hospitality and live among them. All they were to ask in return was hospitality and peace.

In the historic churches, we often get tangled up in what comes next, after we go off two by two, and meet people, and offer them peace, and receive their peace in return, and stay at their houses and eat their food. We leap ahead—way ahead—to the part about announcing that the kingdom of God has come near. At this point, members of historic churches start worrying that people will think we are Jesus freaks or associate us with the guy on the corner with his hand-lettered sign and bullhorn. We don't want to be weird or offensive; we want to keep it classy. While it is certainly true that the church has taken the command to be fishers of men too far on many occasions— hooking people with tempting bait, only to drag them out of the water and eat them for dinner—our obsession with keeping things classy is probably a far bigger present-day obstacle to neighborliness than anything we might be tempted to shout on a street corner. For now, I will permit you to leave your bullhorn at home. There is plenty to do before you get to the point where you might need to use it.

Take it one step at a time. Let's start by going where the people are and finding some respectful ways to learn about and enter into their lives. Let's bring some peace, and maybe receive some in return. Let's eat some good food, even if we have to cook it or buy it ourselves to get started. That in itself may be enough to get the conversation going about the good things that God is up to. Or we may receive further instruction a little farther down the road.

Let's start with pilgrimage. I am a serious believer in the power of pilgrimage. I have never been to the Holy Land or walked the Camino de Santiago. But I have been to the Manzanar War Relocation Center and also to Japan, Korea, El Salvador, and Mexico. I've stood in front of the Basilica de Guadalupe as supplicants crawled past me on their knees. I've walked to the border fence in California and stood on both banks of the Rio Grande/Bravo in Texas and Mexico. I've ridden buses and trains and driven empty roads. I've walked on a lot of broken sidewalks. I've stood on the holy ground where Oscar Romero and other martyrs of the Salvadoran civil war were killed. I've sat with an LA parishioner's mother in her home in rural El Salvador and heard the story of her children leaving one after another to head for safety in the United States during El Salvador's civil war.

Not all my pilgrimages have involved travel. But they have all been about stepping into another place, a place that is not entirely my own, one where I feel unsure and see and smell and taste and sense things that offer glimpses into the lives of people whose experience differs greatly from my own. I've read memoirs and novels and interviews, watched movies and documentaries, wandered grocery store aisles, visited apartments only blocks from my church and my home. There are many ways to enter into other experiences.

Pilgrimage is different from study. I grew up in an academic family and community. The default answer for any question that had to do with learning was study. Want to learn more about some particular group that inhabits your surroundings? Ask an expert. Better yet, become an expert.

There is much to be learned from academic study and reading. But if we are learning in order to build relationships, the academic model of expertise has its limits. It is possible to know a great deal about your neighbors without actually knowing your neighbors or entering into their experience. It is even possible for academic knowledge or expertise to interfere with your ability to build relationships.

I've spent my life in mostly multicultural situations and my ministry as a white pastor in multiethnic communities. I have asked some stupid questions and some smart ones. I have come to recognize diversity as complex, a never-ending unpacking of layers of detail and human experience. I have learned the hard way that no amount of study will make me an expert on someone else's life or someone else's community. I have found that the ability to ask good questions, and to tread lightly, is far more useful in building relationships and community than any level of expertise.

All of this has led me to place pilgrimage at the center of my pastoral practice. When I have questions, I seek and find ways to take pilgrimage, to go deeper, to be more than a tourist. I am constantly inviting others to undertake pilgrimage with me. I understand pilgrimage broadly. As rector at St. Mary's, I have undertaken journeys on foot, by car, and by plane but also into books, movies, corner markets, community events, and my own kitchen, seeking to deepen my knowledge of the lives of my neighbors. I distinguish between pilgrimage and study: pilgrimage seeks to open my eyes and ears, generating good questions and helping me to hear the answers. Pilgrimage does not make me an expert in the lives of others.

Here is a story of pilgrimage from my context at St. Mary's.

It was early December when I set out for the Manzanar War Relocation Center, now known as the Manzanar National Historic Site. Los Angeles was gray and drizzly when I left. As I

headed northeast, the weather quickly turned colder. The road—
even seventy years after the expulsion of all people of Japanese
ancestry from their West Coast homes and communities—is isolated. Beautiful and forbidding desert landscape stretches as far as
the eye can see. I traveled through scrubby sagebrush, an ancient
lava field, a canyon of red rocks. The towns were small and bleak.
I passed a huge field of jet plane parts, stored in an area where
space is no object. Snow flurries picked up as I headed north.
When I checked into my motel in Lone Pine, not much of the
landscape was visible. The gray of the sky seemed to reach to the
ground, and only a few misty hills framed the background.

My first afternoon at Manzanar was bone chilling, my LA winter gear no match for the swirling wind. I walked around a bit,
entered the reconstructed barracks and dining hall on the site—a
single square mile—that had for a few years housed 10,000 Japanese Americans, behind barbed wire and guarded by soldiers in
watchtowers. Mostly, I retreated to the heated museum, poring
over records and testimony, photographs and scratchy film footage. The picture that emerged was overwhelming, enlighten-
ing, and terribly sad. Two images stuck with me that afternoon,
both having to do with children. One was a film of children from
Manzanar's elementary school, dressed in American colonial costume, reenacting America's bid for freedom. The other was a set
of pictures from the Manzanar orphanage. Japanese American
orphans, no matter how young, whether or not they were living
with Japanese families, were pulled from the institutions and fos-
ter homes where they lived and sent to camp along with everyone
else. If anything brought home the racial determinism of internment, these orphan children were it. Any pretense of protecting
the nation from adults with potential dual loyalties or protecting Japanese Americans from overzealous patriots came undone
with the images of these children, too young even to know why
they were uprooted from their already fragile circumstances and
placed in an orphanage inside a prison.

I ate dinner alone at one of the few restaurants in Lone Pine
and went to bed early. The next morning, I stepped out of my
room. The sun was out. Towering in the near distance—where

the day before there had been only gray—were Mount Whitney and the spectacular peaks of the high Sierra. It was even colder than the day before, but the view was dazzling. As I drove back to Manzanar for further exploration, I marveled at the austere beauty of the site. I could see how the modifications that the residents had made to the camp—things like the placement of the park and the graveyard—were created with the mountain peaks as a backdrop. I walked the length and width of the camp. I read all the signs and examined the ruins. The place has been largely abandoned since the war. Rusty nails and old tin cans and the remains of foundations and concrete structures still give testimony to the lives that were lived there seven decades before.

Why the pilgrimage to Manzanar? I went because I am a white woman priest called to serve a century-old congregation, founded by the first generation of Japanese immigrants to California, and still populated in part by their children and grandchildren and great-grandchildren. I went because the internment story is woven into Japanese American identity, even for those who did not live the history firsthand. I went because I knew a little bit about that history but not nearly enough. I went so that I could hear the fragments of stories that would come to me in serving St. Mary's without having to ask people to start at the very beginning. I went so that I could read a bit of what is between the lines in the culture and practice of my church.

I chose this particular part of Japanese American history to make my first major St. Mary's-related pilgrimage because internment is literally part of the architecture at St. Mary's. A stained glass window on the north side of our sanctuary depicts Jesus kneeling in the garden of Gethsemane. He offers up a chalice; it hovers just above his hands. In the upper part of the window, the pillar of cloud and fire from the exodus appears. Around the edges are the diocesan shields of each of the Episcopal dioceses in whose territory the internment camps were built. At the bottom is a memorial to the Nisei soldiers' units from World War II. At the back of the church hangs a framed copy of the evacuation order. St. Mary's address stands out at the center of the document: the assembly point for people of Japanese ancestry living roughly in the square mile surrounding the church. The order includes a very short list of the personal necessities that each family could bring with them. Next to the order is a very short letter of apology from the first President George Bush. It was sent out with the reparation checks received by Japanese Americans after a powerful advocacy campaign in the early 1990s.

The pilgrimage to Manzanar was an essential part of my first year at St. Mary's. Someday I may go back with members of my congregation, both Japanese American and not. I needed to go alone for the first visit. I needed to pray in that broken place, and to hear those long-ago voices, and to touch a tiny piece of the history that still looms large in the church I have been called to serve.

I didn't go so that I could tell St. Mary's about my trip. Most of my Japanese American parishioners have made their own pilgrimages to Manzanar or to the places where they or their families were interned. Some groups, such as those interned at Heart Mountain in Wyoming, hold reunions and keep in touch. Few of St. Mary's parishioners actually spent time at Manzanar itself when it was open. The people in the immediate neighborhood of the church, including St. Mary's priests at the time, went to other camps in Arizona and Arkansas. I didn't go so that I could tell people anything about their experience or their parents' and grandparents' experience that they didn't already know.

I did go because I am St. Mary's priest. I went so that I could enter into the story in a new way. I saw things that made connections for me that I might not have made otherwise. I felt the ghosts of the place in a way that I could not have from a distance. Even the drive brought home the isolation and distance of this, the closest camp to Los Angeles. I didn't know where I was going, exactly, or what it would look like. I glimpsed ever so slightly how the drive into the unknown might have felt to a mother, keeping her children close, determined to make a home for them wherever they ended up out of the few possessions they had been able to bring.

There were lots of little things that shifted after my visit to

Manzanar, more than any one big "aha" moment. One small (small-minded?) example: in my best curmudgeon mode, I had considered sparring with the powers that be at St. Mary's over spending money and energy on large floral arrangements for funerals. The complicated, expensive system by which various St. Mary's organizations got together to provide a large floral cross for each member—however vaguely connected—seemed antiquated, unnecessary, not-so-environmental. At Manzanar, I saw a picture of a funeral, conducted in the camp cemetery with its stark cross and its spectacular view of Mount Whitney. Someone had died at camp—ending their walk on this earth behind barbed wire—and a crowd was there to see them off. Surrounding the coffin were dozens of large floral wreaths. I don't even know how one got large floral wreaths at Manzanar. There was certainly nowhere to grow that many flowers in camp. Did local florists in the tiny towns around camp deliver? In the 1940s? During the war? What must that have cost? Whatever the cost, it was done. I recognized the quiet dignity of a community honoring its dead, no matter the circumstances. I never had that fight about funeral flowers at St. Mary's.

By now, most of the survivors of the internment experience are people who were children during the war. I was impressed by the number of activities at Manzanar that created a semblance of normalcy for kids. This resonates with some of the stories I have heard from people who were children in "camp." It always takes me a minute to translate, "when we went to camp"—away from my own summer camp experiences and toward those windswept barracks, lined up in rows. Some people share memories of childhood in camp as a time of freedom and play. They remember being shielded from at least some of the indignities by zealous parents, learning things from intergenerational gatherings, running wild with friends their own age. Manzanar had dozens of activities for young people—baseball and judo and dances and school plays and graduations and high school yearbooks.

The hard-won shreds of normalcy at Manzanar gave me a new perspective on St. Mary's attachment to normalcy at church. I glimpsed how hard Japanese Americans worked, in camp and after, to show their fellow Americans that they were just people, regular Americans, not to be feared or separated out. I could even see their appreciation for the postwar opportunity just to *be* normal people, to live normal, quiet lives after such traumatic disruption. A full Sunday school and church potlucks with Jell-O salad (even if it was eaten with chopsticks) and homes in the suburbs and kids whose successes in school and sports were judged on their own merits were all a part of this picture. I could begin to imagine why St. Mary's blended so quietly into its environment—an unassuming color, virtually no signs, no clearly marked entrance. After so much unwanted attention, maybe people just wanted a safe place to gather unnoticed by the larger world.

The determination of the residents of Manzanar to create beauty moved me deeply. In a relatively short span of time, even in that inhospitable environment, gardens sprang up. Because Japanese gardens so often involve water and rocks and reshaping the land, the ruined gardens are some of the features that are still easily seen at Manzanar. Each block of barracks had one; certain blocks were famous for their beauty. At the back of the camp, an entire park was constructed. In the pictures, it rivals any lovely city park. Couples strolled and trees bloomed.

St. Mary's exists in a neighborhood that is short on obvious beauty. The well-tended grounds of the church and the members' concerns about neatness and presentability took on new meaning for me after visiting Manzanar. I have begun to encourage St. Mary's consciously to think of itself as a needed place of beauty—that refuge amidst the visible signs of the neighborhood's struggles and neglect. Trees and flowers and careful tending become antidotes to the visual assaults of graffiti and potholes and dumped furniture and litter.

What pilgrimages might you undertake in your ministry context?
Because of my own experience and the context of my ministry, many of my stories and examples have to do with learning and relationship building in the context of racial, ethnic, language, and class diversity. Even in a relatively homogeneous setting—where most people are from similar racial, ethnic, and

class backgrounds—you will find diversity of experience across generational lines, lines of profession and work experience, family organization, and so on. A married woman in her sixties will find important differences in experience between herself and a single mother in her twenties, even if they share a common racial, ethnic, and cultural background. All ministry has elements of relationship building across gaps of experience. All of us need ways to learn more about each other's experience. All of us will have to find ways to offer ourselves and receive offerings from people whose lives are different from ours. Especially for those of us from the dominant culture in our context, it is critical to seek experiences that fire up our imaginations about what it might be like to be further from the center.

Look at your map, the one you made by looking back, looking out, and looking up. Think about what you saw, who you've met in the neighborhood. Who do you know a lot about? Who do you know a little about? Who do you know nothing about? Look beyond the demographic categories for the diversity that exists within categories.

What kinds of things might you try?

Use your senses. What does life smell like in the nooks and crannies of your neighborhood? What does it taste like? What sounds do you hear? What is for sale? What kinds of events gather people?

Travel. I have visited the home countries of several of the large immigrant groups in my neighborhoods and churches. I see what people have brought with them and what they have left behind. I can imagine in new ways what must be hard about the transition. I discover my neighbors as Americans as I experience the ways that they have adapted to their new home.

Don't reserve all your travel for exotic locations. Your neighbors live most of their lives right in your neighborhood. You may learn the most by poking your head into the places where those daily lives take place. This can also be the most intimidating. I have stepped off a plane alone in Korea and found my way to the center of Seoul. That adventure was no match for the intimidation of walking into a small Korean restaurant or store in my neighborhood. White American tourists have a well-established place in Seoul. White American neighbors almost never show up in the corner stores and tiny restaurants of Koreatown. It's OK to be a little uncomfortable as you venture into your neighbors' space. If you feel shy and out of place among your neighbors, there is a good chance they feel the same if they venture into your church's space.

Read books, especially books written by members of the communities you are trying to get to know rather than just about them. Fiction is good, as well as memoir and more academic accounts.

Watch movies. Documentaries are great. Regular old movies are good too. Know the limitations of movies, of fiction. But don't shy away from visual representations of experiences you will share in no other way.

Shop, cook, eat. My neighborhood is full of large Korean and Latino supermarkets as well as smaller markets that cater to specific Latino communities, and to smaller immigrant groups like Bangladeshis. I do a fair amount of shopping outside the neighborhood, at places that carry more of the ingredients I am used to using to stock my kitchen. As I have tried to walk more and drive less, I have made more attempts in recent years to cook with locally available ingredients. I now know the difference between dried mung beans with the skin on and the ones that have the skin off. Turns out skin on your mung beans will spell doom for your *bin dae dduk*. Trust me.

Cook for yourself, but by all means let your neighbors cook for you. Check out the local restaurants, especially the newer ones. Your encounters on church turf will go much better if you bring a little familiarity with what your neighbors like to eat.

What kinds of things might you pay attention to? The wonderful thing about pilgrimage is that some of the things that catch your attention will be things you would never have thought to look for. But it doesn't hurt to have some questions in mind.

Where is the joy in your community? How do people celebrate? What makes them laugh? What do they do to create beauty?

Where is the sorrow in your community? Some communities hide their sorrows better than others, but quiet and persistent observers will see signs of the burdens people carry.

Wonder about this community that lives most of its life without participating in the life of your church. Who are the spiritual leaders? When we see ourselves as volunteering to fill this position, it is easy to miss the spiritual leadership that is right under our noses. If people are not going to church, it does not mean they are not looking to spiritual leaders in important moments. Who comes when someone dies? Who prays with them? For them? Who do they go to when they are spooked? Some of these leaders may be open to partnership. Some won't be. Some of their approaches will be incompatible with your approach. But you still won't go wrong by knowing who they are and showing them respect.

How do people organize themselves? Is your community highly individualized, with everyone pursuing his or her own path? Do people live in nuclear family groups? Extended families? Communities that are defined by shared experience or shared origins or shared interests? Do people hang out mostly with friends or family members? A diverse group of neighbors or mostly people of their own ethnic group or age group?

Within the ways that people organize themselves, who are the leaders? Who represents others in conflicts and crises with the world outside the unit? Who are the trusted outsiders? Which outsiders are not to be trusted?

Pilgrimage helps you ask better questions. It gives you places to start conversations. It opens your mind and your heart and your spirit to other lives and other sacred spaces and other ways of knowing God and being holy.

When you find questions that give people the opportunity to talk about things that they think are important or interesting, they will usually tell you quite a bit. When you ask them as an expert, an investigator, an interrogator—seeking information for your own benefit—they are less likely to respond. Ask to build relationship. Assume that people are experts in their own lives and that you have much to learn.

An NPR story on race featured a young woman of color who offered the challenge: "Ask *who* I am, not *what*." Who are you? Ask not as a specimen study or for the purpose of anthropological description. Ask to generate better questions, and avoid questions that break relationship. (Watch the viral YouTube video "What kind of Asian are you?" for my brother- and sister-in-laws' humorous look at tacky neighbor questions). Most of us hate to be labeled, and yet being mislabeled is probably worse. Asking with love and respect in a way that invites people to share their real selves and their real lives opens a path for relationship.

Chapter Five

Try Things

At the end of forty days Noah opened the window of the
ark that he had made and sent out the raven; and it went
to and fro until the waters were dried up from the earth.
Then he sent out the dove from him, to see if the waters
had subsided from the face of the ground; but the dove
found no place to set its foot, and it returned to him to
the ark, for the waters were still on the face of the whole
earth. So he put out his hand and took it and brought it
into the ark with him. He waited another seven days, and
again he sent out the dove from the ark; and the dove
came back to him in the evening, and there in its beak was
a freshly plucked olive leaf; so Noah knew that the waters
had subsided from the earth. Then he waited another
seven days, and sent out the dove; and it did not return to
him any more.

—Genesis 8:6–12

Several of the communities I have served as a priest celebrate
a second memorial service either forty days after death or at
the one year mark, sometimes both. These services are different
from funerals. The sense of crisis and frenetic activity that sur-
rounds death has passed. Fewer people attend. There is a wider
gap between the grief of the closest friends and family members
and that of others who are there to support them. After forty days

or a year, it matters whether the person was a part of your daily life or only someone you saw occasionally. It can be hard for the closest survivors to witness how quickly and how thoroughly the rest of the world moves on.

This part of the Noah story—about what happens as the flood waters recede—is one of the best ways I have found to reflect pastorally on the long-term experience of grief. Loss reshapes our lives. Death, like a flood, rearranges even the most familiar landmarks, leaving a new landscape for us to navigate. Sooner or later, we get back to our routines, go back home, go back to work, school, shopping, cooking, most of the things that we did before the death of the person we love. But nothing is quite the same. The familiar becomes unfamiliar. Having new experiences, eating new meals, even sharing new joys, feels wrong without the person we have buried. We don't know how or when it is OK to start doing things again. It can feel safer not to venture out of the ark.

Grieving people often find themselves under intense pressure to "move on" or "get back out there." The Noah story suggests a gentler path, yet one that is insistent in its hope. Send out the dove. If there's no dry land yet, just welcome it back. But send it out again. Look for it on the horizon. And when it brings something green, receive the sign. Know that it is time, that the landscape may be unfamiliar, but that the gift of new life is waiting.

Death brings grief, and our churches are dying. So many deaths combine to make up the whole—deaths of individuals we have loved and shared our lives with and also deaths of the ways we have known to do things, to be church. Grief is real and present in our church communities, and its effect should not be discounted. We have loved our churches as they were and loved the people who were there with us. Sometimes we allow ourselves to indulge fantasies of what it would be like if all the loss could just be undone. But most of the time we know, whether we acknowledge it or not, that what is gone is gone. What is to come will be different, new, unfamiliar.

The church's time in the ark—all the decline and loss that we have seen in recent decades, all the change we have seen sweep over the cultural landscape—has not been easy. Grief weighs us down, slows our reflexes, dims our hope. Grief and loss make change seem not just difficult but disloyal. As we peek out of the ark, the landscape looks different, even unrecognizable. It is hard to imagine how we might navigate, much less have something to offer.

In the midst of grief, in the midst of still feeling pretty stuck and unsure, it is time to try things. If you have done some of the things in section 1, especially the mapping work, you should be able to come up with one or two ideas.

Spend some time coming up with your ideas. But not too much time. The ideas should be manageable. They should not assume a wave of neighborhood enthusiasm for church that you have not yet seen. They should in some way reflect what you saw when you looked around.

Here are some questions that might help you come up with things to try:

- What evidence of spirituality did you see among your neighbors? Might you do something that would respond to what you saw?
- What kinds of positive things are your neighbors doing that they look like they could use help with?
- What do your neighbors see when they look at your church? What signals are you sending out?
- Is there something you could build, plant, paint, label or change that might send a signal of readiness for new life and new people?

For God's sake, don't pick all of these things. One or two things will be plenty to start with.

Don't hang all your hopes for the future on these efforts. These are your doves, sent out over a pretty bleak landscape with uncertain return. Some of them will come back empty. Some of them will come back bearing plants you are pretty sure you don't recognize, things that will produce fruit you don't know how to eat.

This is not your strategic plan. These are things you are trying, because you are grieving and uncertain, and you need to send out the dove.

Do pay attention to what comes back. Sometimes it will be subtle. You will have to watch for it. It probably won't be a full church and a balanced budget, so go ahead and let those particular hopes go. Remind other people that it is an experiment. By definition, we don't know what the outcome will be.

St. Mary's has tried a lot of things in recent years, starting well before I arrived on the scene. When I got there, they were disappointed in some of the things they had tried. They were a little frustrated with their neighbors for not understanding and receiving their efforts.

As we have tried things together, I have introduced a concept that we call in my family "adventure spirit." We coined the term on a vacation day when nothing had gone as planned. Having to scrap the adventure we had looked forward to, we headed out without a clear destination and agreed that we would just see what came. We reminded each other that everyone would have to be a little patient and that no one would have all the answers to the usual questions: "Are we there yet?" and "What are we going to eat?" Now almost every time we head out to do something new together, someone in the family will say, "Adventure spirit?" We are each expected to answer in the affirmative, signaling our commitment to meet the day together.

Because my family is made of real people, not television actors, not everyone is always equally committed to adventure spirit. Some days one or more of us is grumpy, hungry, sad, or just not in the mood for what we end up eating for lunch. Sometimes we commit to adventure spirit in the morning, but by afternoon, we are tired of new things and would like everyone and everything to give us a break. You should expect this to be true in church as well.

Here are a few adventures we have tried in recent years at St. Mary's.

The Guadalupe Shrine

If Los Angeles has a patron, it is the Virgin of Guadalupe. Her image is everywhere—on the sides of stores, on pendants around people's necks, inside and outside people's homes in Latino neighborhoods and beyond. About a mile from St. Mary's, right on the walking route between the church and my house, there is a Guadalupe shrine outside a private home. The small brick alcove, with its painted plaster Guadalupe statue, receives dozens of visitors a day. Votive candles burn constantly, placed by neighbors who have come to pray. Fresh flowers and little notes and photos are further evidence of the devotion of passers-by. There is often someone sitting on the bench near the shrine or kneeling before the Virgin and her candles. People bring their kids to teach them to pray.

By the time I got there, St. Mary's had a statue of Guadalupe in the church but nothing on the outside. I showed people pictures of the shrine near my house and suggested we try something similar. When one of our community garden projects presented the opportunity to create an outdoor prayer space, we created a small stone altar and attached an image of Guadalupe. We installed it just before her feast day on December 12, which happened to fall on a Sunday that year.

Whenever I get frustrated with St. Mary's longtime members and the resistance they occasionally show in the face of change— whenever I fault their adventure spirit—I remember how many of them stood outside with me on that drizzly December morning, did their best to sing along with the traditional *mañanitas*, and blessed this image that we offered to our neighborhood. I know that not all of them were sure what we were doing or why I thought this was worthwhile. Despite my sincere and sometimes long-winded attempts to tell the story of Guadalupe, they were not at all clear what it was about. But they were ready to try this, to trust (or indulge) their new priest enough to see what would happen.

So we tried it. And sure enough, our Guadalupe began to show signs of use. Candles emerged, and small offerings: pictures and decorations and potted plants. Around her feast day, or other major feasts, fresh flowers would appear. It wasn't on the scale of the one by my house, but our Guadalupe was becoming a place of prayer. Several smaller Guadalupes have joined the original large image, including my personal favorite: an image in velvet of the Virgin herself presiding over a lowrider car show.

Over time, we were inconsistent in our care of the site. As we got busy with the actual neighbors who showed up at church, this early outreach attempt seemed less central. Sometimes no one would tend to the space for several weeks. Flowers would wilt and dry, and candles would shatter their cheap glass housing. Someone—usually me—would remember and scurry out to clean up, embarrassed that we had let it go so long. And then someone began taking care of it. Every day. Nothing huge, just straightening, and neatening, and picking up trash. We didn't know who it was for the longest time. Community gardeners said it was a man from the apartments across the street.

We didn't meet Guadalupe's caretaker until this past December 12, when another series of experiments led us to do a proper day-of celebration of the Guadalupe feast in the evening at the church. The mariachi band was easily heard across the street. Our neighbor attended the service and identified himself at the end. He was pleased with the celebration and pleased with our display of the outdoor image. We haven't seen him at church since, but the evidence of his care and of our neighbors' private prayer lives remain, day by day.

The Murals

Another thing we tried was letting a group of graffiti artists spray-paint the walls, both in and outside the church. This worked surprisingly well.

It started with a teacher from a local school for students ages eighteen to twenty-four who had not completed traditional high school programs and were now trying to make up credits toward graduation. The teacher was looking for internship and service opportunities for his students. In the spirit of saying "yes" (see the next chapter), I brainstormed with him about what his students might be able to do at the church. When I mentioned the dream of having some mural art on our large blank walls, his face lit up. He loves mural art, and he knew that several of the students spent a lot of their time doing art, sometimes at the expense of their homework.

The teacher brought a group of students to look at the wall I had in mind. It was a long blank corridor, leading to our office. It was tall, probably fifteen feet. They eyed it. We discussed possible themes. Then they asked what kind of materials they would use. I'm no artist. I think my answer was, "Uh . . . paint, like with brushes?" They contemplated. Finally one of them asked how I felt about spray. I said I didn't have anything against spray, but it seemed like more of an outdoor paint. I couldn't picture using spray indoors, what with fumes and mess and so on. Plus I didn't really want the corridor leading to the church office to look like full-on graffiti. They mentioned that they had seen spray used indoors, but politely acknowledged my concerns. At our next meeting, however, one of them spoke up more firmly. "You know, we mostly work in spray." He suggested we try just a small patch, see how the smell was, and experiment with rigging up adequate ventilation. And so we did. He happened to have a can of paint in his pocket. Right there on our clean wall, he sketched a green spray-paint bird.

To make a long story short, we now have not one, but three spray-painted murals, one indoors and two outdoors. They are beautiful. They are almost finished, as they have been for quite a while. The lead artist has gotten a job, which means he shows up inconsistently, but he shows up. He is so taken with the project that he tends to start new elements rather than finish ones that need touching up, seeing the spaces as a never-ending canvas for his creativity.

Not everyone at St. Mary's loves the murals, but most people are pretty enthusiastic. I find younger members of the church, home from college or back to visit from out of town, admiring the work and showing it to one another. At the Sunday service when we unveiled the first mural, we presented the artists with a certificate. Their school principal came, and one student invited his mother. He said it was the first time she had ever seen him recognized for something good he had done.

Looking back, this engagement with talented youth in our

neighborhood and the resulting addition of color and creativity to our space seems like a no-brainer. But when people ask, "How did you know it would turn out so well?" I give the honest answer, "I didn't." It could have looked terrible. It could have made a mess. The students could have quit mid-project. The content could have been inappropriate. All of these things were possible, even foreseeable. We got lucky. But what if we hadn't? We would have cleaned up and painted over the walls, and moved on. It would have been a while before the church board would have approved another art project. But so what? The blessings of this project have been much greater than the downside risk. It was so worth a try.

Open Church

Some of the things we have tried have worked better than others, at least initially. I have a fantasy of having a church that is always open for prayer. I believe that everyone should have a quiet holy place to be at peace with their thoughts, their prayers, and their sorrows. St. Mary's, like most Episcopal churches, was locked up tight as Fort Knox every minute that there wasn't worship happening in the sanctuary. At first I thought we'd get some volunteers to watch over things. When that seemed easier said than done, I wondered if we could just leave it open whenever there was staff in the building, even without anyone to watch the sanctuary directly. What would happen? I suspected that our neighbors would care for our holy space and be glad to have it available. I was willing to take the risk.

We tried it. We did lock up a few things—silver, brass, and sound equipment. I'm a savvy enough urban dweller and priest to know that some things are mighty temptations. Here's what happened: almost everybody was deeply respectful of the space. No one slept on the pews or peed in the corners or attacked anyone else or tagged the walls. No one stole anything. But one guy did start coming in and roaming around the building. He made spectacular messes in the kitchen. He left drug paraphernalia in the bathroom. He surprised people, and not in a good way, popping out of dark corners unexpectedly.

By the end of a single week, we could see that it wasn't working. So we stopped. But the whole experience eventually inspired some of the same neighbors who were most enthusiastic about having the church open to volunteer to be there to watch over things. So it's open. Not all the time, not every day. But most days, for a few hours in the morning. And people come. There's a key attached to the railing by the entrance with one of those combination real estate locks. The volunteers take out the key, open the doors, and sit in the entryway embroidering, or polish the pews, or practice singing or playing the piano. Everyone has their own style. They watch out for things. It turns out we needed that.

Trying things without any real expectation about how they will work goes against our instincts in the church. We want to appear successful, in control. We want to *be* in control. We would often rather do nothing than appear foolish.

Trying things makes us vulnerable, leaves us open to rejection. The things we try may seem stupid or not make sense to the people around us. It is exactly that vulnerability and willingness to look foolish that leads to new sorts of relationships, better relationships, just the sorts of relationships that will give us the courage to face death and resurrection. Our open imperfection gives courage to other imperfect people to approach, to make suggestions. It opens us to the ministry of others, who may just be able to help us when we acknowledge we need it.

Trying things is good practice for our imagination. Imagining good things happening is a first step in opening ourselves to what God may be up to. It is easy to feel like we have tried everything, seen everything—that our best days are behind us. With God, there is always something up ahead, even when we seem to have reached the end of the road. Trying things gives testimony to that faith. Even if we can't see it, we believe there is more still to come, blessings as yet unreceived, possibilities still untested. So send out that dove.

Chapter Six

Say Yes

At some point, if they see signs of openness, your neighbors will also start coming to you. Be warned that you may miss it. They will probably not come in the way that you had hoped they would: attending church or seeking spiritual guidance. They may very well want practical things that do not seem particularly church related, and they may show up at inconvenient times. They may have strange requests. They may not tell you what they actually want. All of these things have happened in my experience.

Here's what I think you should do absolutely any time you can: *say yes*. Unless there is some really compelling threat to life and limb if you say yes, just say it. Even if you're not sure it's a good idea. Even if you don't think it will do anything to build the church. Even if you're not sure why anyone would want to do whatever it is your neighbors are up to. Even if you've never done anything like it before. Even if it involves loaning out keys to people you don't know very well. Even if it might leave a mess. Even if you might have to clean it up. Even if you're not sure that everyone in the church will think it is a good idea.

If you can't say yes to the exact request before you, think about what you could say yes to. Then say yes to that. If you can't say yes without consulting someone else, explain how that process works and why, and let people know how long it will take (and make sure it is not months or years). Show your neighbors that you want to work with them, that you want to say yes, that you and your congregation are ready to offer yourselves. Throw caution to the wind, and expect that your neighbors will offer themselves in return. That they will take good care of the building. That they will clean up. That they will help you solve the problems that will from time to time arise. That they will do interesting things that will have meaning to their own families and communities— things that you might not have thought of. That what they are doing now might not be the last thing they will ever do at your church. That there might be the seeds of a relationship buried in a utilitarian request.

There is a Hebrew way of saying yes. It is "Hineni." Here I am.

> Then I heard the voice of the Lord saying, "Whom shall I send, who will go for us?" And I said, "Here am I, send me!" (Isaiah 6:8)

Most churches default to "no" most of the time. Locked doors say no. Long lists of requirements say no. Enormous security deposits say no. Overly restrictive policies about who can have keys say no. Dirty looks say no. Prudence and due diligence often say no.

Most of the time, when we say no, we say it out of fear. Beware that fear often masquerades as caution and good sense. We say no because we can imagine that things might go badly. It's so important that we practice using our imaginations for good—imagining what miracles God might work with our small offerings rather than dwelling on possible calamity. However, we are humans. Our imaginations often work toward the negative rather than the miraculous. And sometimes things do go wrong.

If worst comes to worst, and you said yes, and things went badly, here is what you do. Clean up and move on. If someone screws up badly, you have permission to say no to that particular person next time they ask or set some conditions for greater accountability. If some particular type of event or project goes badly, you can set additional limits the next time someone else asks to do something similar. You can tell them what went wrong last time and ask how you can work together so that it will go better this time. In all but the most calamitous of circumstances— which are really pretty rare—this is the sum total of response that is required when a "yes" becomes a mess. If we allow the possibility of calamity to govern our actions, we are in trouble, especially at this rather late stage of the game.

Saying yes is not an easy practice. It's one I am still growing into. I have some people around who know about and share my commitment to saying yes. Whenever I find myself tempted to say no or already having said it, I check with them. They are often able to talk me back around to a yes of some sort. Of all the things I do, saying yes is the one that makes my fellow leaders, our congregation, and our staff the most nervous. Saying yes requires a constant process of checking our instincts. But it is also probably the single most important thing that has opened up life at St. Mary's and set us on the road to a new life as a community church for whatever years we have left.

Here's what I think is really happening when your neighbors show up. You have let God know you are ready. You have gotten up. You've turned out your pockets and offered at least some of what is in there. God has taken you at your word (and seen the rest of what is still in your pockets). God has sent opportunity your way. God has found the people who need what you have. God may have even found the people who have what you need. And God has dropped them on your doorstep. I don't have any other way of explaining some of the people who have arrived on my church doorsteps over the years.

Here's the thing, though. I have not always recognized these gifts when I have received them. I have sometimes held out for better gifts, or different gifts, or gifts that just seem a little bit less odd or a little bit more like a sure thing. The blessings that have come from saying yes have been so strange and wonderful, so life-changing for me and my congregations, that I look back and shake my head at all the gifts I have turned away. I imagine with some sadness the wonders they might have brought.

There's an old joke about God sending help in a flood. The way I learned the joke, the person starts out on the first floor of her house, and it's raining hard. A rescue worker knocks at the door, says the floodwaters are rising, and offers a ride to safety. The person declines, saying that she knows God will keep her safe. The next scene is on the second floor of the house, and the rescuer comes in a boat. The first floor is now underwater. The person declines again, preferring to depend only on God for salvation. The third scene is on the roof. A helicopter hovers above, dangling a precarious-looking hook that could haul the stranded person to safety. She shouts upward, "I still trust that God will save me!" The final scene is at the throne of God. The person demands an explanation for her untimely demise. God throws up the Divine hands in exasperation: "I sent a car . . . I sent a boat . . . I sent a helicopter! What in heaven's name were you waiting for?"

Some of our churches have been waiting at least until the helicopter stage. The only help left feels awfully perilous, maybe almost as dangerous as the rising waters. We have waited for children and then grandchildren to come back. We have waited for the neighborhood to change. We have waited for nice middle-class church-going folks who are ready to fill out a pledge card. We have waited for people who appreciate what we think of as the "right" way of doing things.

Stop waiting. Start saying yes on the off chance that whoever comes to the door might somehow be linked to you in God's plan of salvation. Let's be clear. It isn't your neighbors' job to save your church. Whatever your neighbors bring your way will probably not be the solution to all the problems you've been wanting to solve. You may in fact not get to solve those problems. But if the most faithful way to live out your remaining years is to love God and your neighbor, it sure would be helpful to have some neighbors around, pretty much no matter what they might be up to. So say yes. Let people in. Risk losing control. Risk a few beans clogging the kitchen sink (true story).

Serving as a priest in Latino communities in Los Angeles over more than a decade, I have celebrated quite a few services for *quinceañeras*—girls turning fifteen. The standard format includes a mass, attended mostly by family and close friends, followed by a lavish and much-better-attended party. I have the girls help plan the mass, including picking their own readings. From the list of choices I present, the far-and-away favorite Gospel lesson is the story of the Samaritan woman at the well, from the Gospel of John.

> A Samaritan woman came to draw water, and Jesus said to her, "Give me a drink." (His disciples had gone to the city to buy food.) The Samaritan woman said to him, "How is it that you, a Jew, ask a drink of me, a woman of Samaria?" (Jews do not share things in common with Samaritans.) Jesus answered her, "If you knew the gift of God, and who it is that is saying to you, 'Give me a drink,' you would have asked him, and he would have given you living water." The woman said to him, "Sir, you have no bucket, and the well is deep. Where do you get that living water? Are you greater than our ancestor Jacob, who gave us the well, and with his sons and his flocks drank from it?" Jesus said to her, "Everyone who drinks of this water will be thirsty again, but those who drink of the water that I will give them will never be thirsty. The water that I will give will become in them a spring of water gushing up to eternal life." The woman said to him, "Sir, give me this water, so that I may never be thirsty or have to keep coming to draw water." (John 4:7–15)

Fourteen-year-old girls get a lot of messages about things to which they should (must!) say no. My own daughter's seventh-grade *Teen Health* book spent page after page on "refusal skills." No drugs, no sex, no alcohol, no risks. Say no, say no, say no, say no! I push my quinceañera candidates (and my own daughters) to seek the things to which they will say yes.

The Samaritan woman, in her encounter with Jesus, has several doubts. She is a truth-teller, refusing to gloss over points of cognitive and cultural dissonance. She asks Jesus several pointed questions. What are you, a Jewish man, doing talking to me, a Samaritan woman? How is it that you are going to share my water, when Jews and Samaritans are too deeply divided by culture and history and religion to share food and drink? And how do you plan to get this water, when the well is deep and you have no bucket? She is deeply skeptical, focused on obstacles and the ridiculous premise of Jesus' request. She doesn't refuse the request but inquires, "How is this possible?"

In the midst of her skeptical and gutsy line of questioning, the bucket-less, Jewish Jesus manages to say something that stops her in her tracks, shifting the whole conversation. He speaks of living water, water that will quench her deepest thirst, water that will never run dry. She listens. Her first response comes from a place of practicality: "Give me this water that I may never have to fetch from the well again." That first skeptical yes opens something much deeper than the desire to be free from the onerous task of obtaining water for daily use. Give me that water. The woman hears something life-giving. She is seen for who she is. By the end of the conversation she understands that Jesus is the Messiah. Give me that water.

God offers living water. God offers life, not death. But the water does not always come in the form we expect or from the people we have hoped would help us get it. Give me that water. Our role is to seize that which bears the possibility of new life, that which may quench our deepest thirst. Ours is not to understand the mechanism by which the water comes nor to know the whole story of how the drink of water will lead into eternal life. Ours is to recognize the life that is on offer and seize it.

When strange opportunities present themselves, our better judgment and our judgmental peers often warn against throwing caution to the wind. If the disciples had been there minding Jesus, they might have staged an intervention. If the Samaritan woman had been closely enough connected to her family and community to come in the morning to draw water with the rest of the women, they no doubt would have shielded her from the advances of this strange foreign man. A lot of messy circumstances had to align for this particular conversation to happen.

Dying to our old ways of seeking water means trusting something new and hard to understand. It means risking saying yes every time we even suspect that God may be offering something new. It means having conversations we wish we weren't having, it means letting caution fly out the door, it means proclaiming that Jesus is Lord, and expecting that to mean something, to save us.

Here is a story about saying yes. It took place about a year into my time at St. Mary's, at a point when things looked pretty discouraging on the church survival front. St. Mary's main efforts to reach out to its neighbors—a Spanish-language Sunday service and a community garden—were both struggling. Despite having been around for five or more years, they required a lot of care and feeding from the staff and yielded little of the new membership and participation in church life that people had hoped for. None of the brilliant new ideas and efforts that I had brought with me had had much effect either.

The doorbell rang, which requires someone to leave the office and walk down a long hallway. Our office administrator made the trek and brought two men back to the office. They came reluctantly and stayed close to the exit. When I greeted them in Spanish, they brightened a little, relieved to see one obstacle fall away. One of them took a deep breath and began to mumble a request. They wondered—just a favor, a small thing really—they knew that sometimes people practiced dancing in our parking lot. They were starting a dance group—well it was started already really— it was traditional dancing for kids and they thought maybe they could practice in the parking lot. I said I imagined we could work something out. They looked at each other, gathering courage. The thing was that kids so often need to go to the bathroom. You just get there and start to dance, and there it is, the bathroom problem. Kids, you know.

The parking lot was one thing—large, by urban standards, unlocked, mostly unused in the afternoons and evenings. But bathrooms are indoor amenities. Indoor means keys. Bathrooms can get messy in a hurry, especially when kids are involved. I was pretty new at St. Mary's and had yet to give a key to anyone who wasn't already deeply connected to the church. I hesitated.

Well, I said, keys are a difficult thing. One has to be quite responsible with keys. Who would be watching these kids when they were inside, locking and unlocking doors?

Strangely, my hesitation seemed to give them confidence. That was no problem. No problem at all. It would be members of their community, and their community was reliable. Their community was no trouble at all. Parents and teachers would be watching their children, and they would show me that I had made the right choice to trust them with keys.

This flash of pride and confidence intrigued me. "Where is your community from?" The answer, "Oaxaca!" named the state in southern Mexico, largely populated by tight-knit communities that have hung onto their native traditions and languages through the half-millennium since the Spanish conquest. Oaxaca is the home from which many of our neighbors have come; they almost always identify when asked as being Oaxacan rather than simply Mexican. My visitors stood firm on the solid ground of community pride. It was the right question, one that brought light to their eyes.

I agreed to consider their request, gave them a form to fill out, and asked them to bring it back in a few days. I told them I would have to consult with my leaders about the keys. We exchanged names and phone numbers. Their gratitude was disproportionate to my rather limited generosity on behalf of the church, and it made them talkative. They were just representatives, really, and they had a community president who made all final decisions. He would be the one to review the paperwork. There was a dance teacher too, very experienced and responsible. A whole community danced just offstage as they talked.

I almost said no. I was new, barely a year into ministry with a congregation that counts time in decades. Stewardship of property and keys was closely guarded at St. Mary's, as at most churches, and no one had unsupervised access except longtime members, staff and paying tenants. In the lore of the congregation were one or two community events gone wrong. It may really just have been one event: a quinceañera that ended in some unspecified disaster. (Noise complaint to the police? Scratches on the wooden floor from heavy DJ equipment? Poor cleanup? All of the above? The details have been lost to history.) Giving out keys willy-nilly to people I barely knew was sure to attract skepticism at best. I did it anyway, in this case without much consulting. I decided I was willing to explain myself later whether things went well or not. At the time, I had not yet articulated this spirituality of saying yes. If you are a part of your congregation's leadership team, you have a great opportunity: empower whoever is around to receive your neighbors to say yes to reasonable requests without an overly complicated process of consultation. Offer a wide margin of grace when errors of judgment or unpleasant surprises occur. Take a deep breath and believe that there will be more blessings than disasters.

I learned later that the emissaries from the dance group had almost run away. They had stood at the door and thought this had not been a good idea. They had seriously considered just making a run for it and telling their president that no one had answered. I'm awfully glad they didn't run away. I'm equally glad that I came as close to yes as I did.

Two years later, the community represented by these two shy messengers is a vibrant part of life at St. Mary's. Members of their community are present at the church nearly every day. Their youth band practices upstairs. The dancers have long since migrated from the parking lot to the more pleasant and shady courtyard. The community tuba lives in our basement, and the kids' basketball team practices in our parking lot. The town council meets in our empty classrooms, and food for the community's festivals is prepared in our kitchen.

And yes . . . they come to church. Some of them, anyway, some of the time. The statue of their hometown's patron saint stands near the church entrance, lovingly adorned with fresh flowers and candles. The scent of copal—traditional Mesoamerican incense—lingers in the air of the sanctuary. It is people from their community who keep the church open on weekday mornings so that people can come inside to pray. They hold rosary services on Sunday evenings that draw hundreds of people. The youth band plays for special church services. Seeing these activities, other Oaxacan communities have begun to approach. We have two more bands, more dancers, more community meetings.

How we got from there to here is a long story. Much is still to be revealed about where we are all going together. But it started with a small request, one that had nothing to do with worship or the sharing of spiritual life. A strange and wonderful tree has grown out of a yes the size of a mustard seed—a tree that looks nothing like what either St. Mary's or this small community from the mountains of Oaxaca has ever known before. We are building a relationship—one that is not without bumps, but one that is based on mutual respect and gratitude, mutual honesty and vulnerability, mutual offering of gifts, mutual willingness to try new things.

One of the things that I have learned from this still-unfolding story is that spirituality is intimate, often closely guarded. It will rarely be the first question, the first approach. Saying yes to all remotely feasible requests opens the door for friendship, for building confidence and community. Saying yes tells us what our neighbors are looking for and tells them that we value the community and family celebrations and activities they value.

Puzzling as it may seem from inside the church, our neighbors may well have complex spiritual lives that they have not considered situating in a church community. When they first eye the church, it is often for purposes that are not explicitly spiritual. Our challenge, in part, is to take a more holistic view of spirituality. But we also should not expect that we can wait for people to arrive asking after what we would most like to offer. Even if our hearts' desire is to share the Good News (and this should be our hearts' desire), we should not assume that the only way to do that is to have people's first trip inside be to a worship service.

In the case of the Oaxacan community that approached us, the first yes mattered. It was a small yes, grudgingly given. But the triumph of the asking and the opening of that first door mattered. Ms. Emma the administrator hauling them down the hall into the office mattered. My being there and listening respectfully mattered. The fact that I spoke Spanish mattered. The request was not the question all struggling churches are hoping to hear: "We'd like to come and be part of your church; how can we do that?" It was a small request, testing the waters, for something not in any way directly related to the religious purpose of the church. But for a community used to hearing no, this tiny yes was a beginning, the opening of a door. They had not run away, and I had not said no.

Churches spend a lot of time wondering how to reach out to their neighbors. Requests to use space are by far the most common way that St. Mary's neighbors reach out to us. Our church occupies a good share of a block in a neighborhood that is starved for space. Population density in our low-rise neighborhood rivals parts of Manhattan. Ninety-five percent of our neighbors rent their housing, leaving few in full control of even their own living space. The local park is a tangle of rules with little space available to activities not sponsored by the park itself. Local schools lock their gates at night, afraid of liability and graffiti and gang activity. Everyone—from dance groups to skateboarders to kids looking for private spots to smoke pot—roams the neighborhood with an eye out for usable space.

Like so many struggling urban churches, space is one thing we do have in relative abundance: a parking lot, empty Sunday school classrooms, scraps of empty land, our beautiful sanctuary. Some of the space is a little funky—dark, with suspicious smells and stains embedded in the carpets and old posters of blue-eyed Jesus semi-permanently affixed to the walls. Like most churches, we rent out some space. Keeping the whole building in decent shape is an ongoing struggle.

Saying yes to requests for space is always a little risky. Will people care for the property? Will they remember to lock up? Will they take our hospitality for granted, not stopping to consider the central Christian purpose of the church? Will they become the next generation to invest in the facility with love, or will they just leave the place a little more run down than it was when they arrived?

Requests for space reveal a lot about what our neighbors are up to. In our case, the greatest hunger is for dance and music and sports. Our neighbors dance up a storm. Young people practice routines to contemporary music. Older generations impart dance traditions from their homelands. Enthusiastic instructors drag *quinceañera* participants through the motions of traditional waltzes. When live music accompanies dance, it too needs a place to be learned and practiced. Thirty or so elementary-age children arrive every Sunday afternoon at St. Mary's to learn to read music and play the recorder. They hope to graduate to the collection of clarinets, saxophones, trumpets, trombones, and tubas that make up the traditional Zapotec band.

Maybe the best part of lending out space is that it gives our neighbors the chance to minister to one another. Unlike programs that we may offer as a church, the dance groups, bands, and basketball teams are gifts of the neighborhood to itself. Local leaders work on their own time to make these things happen, offering themselves for the benefit of their own communities.

St. Mary's practices a mix of lending, renting, and giving space. When we partner with an organization that has access to funds—for example our Head Start preschool—we charge rent and enter a formal lease agreement. In another case, we offered land free of charge to a group with funding to build and organize community gardens. In the case of individuals and small communities, we generally ask mostly for in-kind contributions of maintenance and participation in parish workdays and events. This has been especially important in creating ties between the people using our space during the week and our longtime members who are mostly around on Sundays. There's nothing like cleaning out the kitchen together to signal common purpose, even across chasms of language and culture.

The bottom line is this: When God sends us new people, our answer needs to be yes. These are our chances, much as we might like those chances to look a little different. These are our opportunities to be a part of the lives of the people we seek to engage.

Saying yes is not just about keys and parish halls and trusting someone else to take out the trash. It starts there. But it is about something more. It is about seizing every bit of life that comes our way and trusting that somewhere in the messiness is the resurrection we long for.

Section Three

A New Country

You've gotten up. You've gotten moving. If you have done those things—whether using the practices I suggest or others you have developed in your own context—you are in a new country. You have probably (hopefully) seen some glimpses of new life along the way. You may have encountered gifts that were entirely unexpected, well beyond what you might have imagined. By all means, celebrate those glimpses. Have fun with the gifts. Enjoy the people who have taken the journey with you and the ones who have shown up along the way. Show your joy abundantly. At the same time, remember where we are going. The new country in which we find ourselves is closer to death and also to what lies beyond. As we move, we gradually close the door on what has gone before. As the small deaths multiply, we edge closer to the end of what we have held most dear, fought for, defended at great cost.

All of these offerings—all these small deaths along the way—give us practice and courage. We grow bolder, more willing to trust the twists and turns of the road. We are not practicing resurrection. Resurrection is God's alone. We walk in the faith that resurrection lies beyond death on the road. We trust that the way will open when we get there.

In Los Angeles, what we see on the horizon depends greatly on the weather and the quality of the air. There are days when we can barely see the tall buildings of downtown, just three miles from the church. We are left with nothing but our immediate surroundings, just a hazy Koreatown cut off from the rest of the world. On better days, we can see downtown, and maybe some of Griffith Park—a surprisingly wild enclave in the hills that run east and west across the middle of LA. With a bit of a view, we become part of a city and an ecosystem that includes coyotes and deer and even a single, much-watched mountain lion. There are hazy days, middle distance days, and then there are great days. Downtown sparkles before a spectacular mountain backdrop. The San Gabriel Mountains are big and steep, and sometimes they have snow. When the air is clear, they are right there, appearing as if out of nowhere to tower over the downtown skyscrapers. On the days when you can see them, it is impossible to believe that the mountains have ever been invisible. On the days when they are obscured, it is equally impossible to believe that they even exist.

Where you are now is like that. There will be days when you can only see a few feet ahead. What you are doing and what you are trying to become will seem uncoupled from any hopeful possibility, any story larger than your own. There will be days when you can see all the way to death but not a foot beyond. But then there will be days when it is dazzlingly clear. The here and now and the death that is to come and the resurrection that lies beyond will be so close that they all seem connected and easy to touch.

Well before Jesus' actual death and resurrection, the disciples began to catch glimpses of the life beyond. The feeding of the multitude is a sure glimpse of a meal at God's table. Remember your sandwich? The story that follows directly after the feeding in the Gospel of Matthew offers another example:

> Immediately [Jesus] made the disciples get into the boat and go on ahead to the other side, while he dismissed the crowds. And after he had dismissed the crowds, he went up the mountain by himself to pray. When evening came, he was there alone, but by this time the boat, battered by the waves, was far from the land, for the wind was against them. And early in the morning he came walking toward them on the sea. But when the disciples saw him walking on the sea, they

were terrified, saying, "It is a ghost!" And they cried out in
fear. But immediately Jesus spoke to them and said, "Take
heart, it is I; do not be afraid." Peter answered him, "Lord,
if it is you, command me to come to you on the water." He
said, "Come." So Peter got out of the boat, started walking on
the water, and came toward Jesus. But when he noticed the
strong wind, he became frightened, and beginning to sink, he
cried out, "Lord, save me!" Jesus immediately reached out his
hand and caught him, saying to him, "You of little faith, why
did you doubt?" (Matt. 14:22–31)

Jesus walks across the water to the boat and the disciples get
a glimpse, a hint that one day the laws of physics and the laws of
life and death as we know them will no longer apply. This is the
super cool news about walking toward death in the hope of resurrection: We get to walk on water. We get to walk on water, defy
the laws of physics, and experience our own taste of eternal life.
This is the not-quite-so-cool news: In the cosmic casting call, we
don't get the part of Jesus. We have to be Peter.

Jesus calls him out of the boat, and Peter goes. Sweet Peter, an
eager beaver, a bit of a show-off, a faithful disciple, an adventurer,
sometimes even a buffoon. He walks across the water. Walks on
the water. Amazing. And then he sinks. Sinks hard. Water up the
nose and all the other disciples watching. He has to be fished out
by Jesus, who cannot resist a little reprimand.

Life in the new country is like that, over and over. We discover
that, when we hold Jesus' gaze and answer his beckoning call,
we can walk on water. We can do things that would have been
impossible not very long ago. I find myself overwhelmed by the
sheer grace that has been visited on our ministry at St. Mary's
as we undertake the practices of faithful dying. Wow. And then
we look down. We have a Sunday when we can hear the crickets
singing along with the hymns. We have one of those epic inter-
cultural misunderstandings that leaves everyone feeling angry
and sad and lonely. We remember who we are and where we are,
and we sink fast and hard.

The chapters in this section are more spiritual and less practical than in the first two sections. They are about what it actually feels like to get out of the boat and walk toward Jesus on the strength of invitation and faith alone. They are about looking down and remembering who we are and where we have been and then promptly forgetting who we are called to be and where we are going. They are about water up our noses and people looking on with interest while we are plucked out of our miserable predicaments and deposited, dripping, back in the boat. They are about what it really looks like to be a church and a people who offer ourselves for death and resurrection.

Here is what I know. It is better to live in the new country than it was to live where you were before. Here is where you will circle inward toward the things that are hardest to let go. Here is where you will glimpse the certainty of your own death and the death of your church and be afraid but walk anyway. Here is where you will find that letting go of survival and success drives us into the center of Christian practice. We have nothing left but the gifts that Jesus gave us: peace and love and forgiveness. Here is where we discover that those gifts are enough.

The three practices in this section are all about the ups and downs of living deeply into these neighborhood-building gifts. "Look Outside the Tent" invites you to give up on doing it yourself, whatever it may be. It reminds you that there are people who are excellent neighbor material out there, probably beyond the boundaries of where you are used to looking. "Expect Trespasses" reminds you not to expect this neighbor business to be simple. "When Faith and Hope Fail, Try Love" is more of a confession, my own story of remembering and re-remembering the call to be neighbor, even when it's not going so well. It's an invitation to go and do likewise, and to know that you are not alone.

These are hard practices, probably as hard or harder than anything you've been trying as you struggled to come up with a plan for success. But unlike strategic plans for institutional survival, these are practices that give life, that draw us closer to God, that reveal God's love and plans and hopes and dreams for us. They are the practices of life on the three-way border between life, death, and eternity.

Chapter Seven

Look Outside the Tent

A family friend is a restaurant critic. He has eaten at a stagger-ing number of the restaurants in greater Los Angeles. If you ask him about any style of food, or any neighborhood, he will have something good to recommend. He commented one day that people always assume that he would never be able to choose a favorite out of all these wonderful eating experiences. Actually, though, he was happy to name just one, a single favorite out of the multitude. (Sorry, foodie Angelenos—the restaurant in question is sadly not there anymore, but man it was good while it lasted.)

I have read the whole Bible quite a few times and preached my share of lectionary cycles. There are too many wonderful things in the Bible to count. But I have one clear favorite, a chapter that I love beyond any and all other parts. It is Numbers 11. For my money, there is no better single story about God and people on the move and the challenges of leadership and the messy grace that ties all three together.

The chapter starts with the people missing home. Home, mind you, was Egypt. Remember Egypt? Pharaoh? Slavery? The mid-wives instructed to kill the babies? But of course those are not the objects of the people's nostalgia. They are missing the food!

The rabble among them had a strong craving; and the Isra-elites also wept again, and said, "If only we had meat to eat!

91

We remember the fish we used to eat in Egypt for nothing, the cucumbers, the melons, the leeks, the onions, and the garlic; but now our strength is dried up, and there is nothing at all but this manna to look at."

Now the manna was like coriander seed, and its color was like the color of gum resin. The people went around and gathered it, ground it in mills or beat it in mortars, then boiled it in pots and made cakes of it; and the taste of it was like the taste of cakes baked with oil. When the dew fell on the camp in the night, the manna would fall with it. (vv. 4–9)

They are complaining about the *manna*, for God's sake, the most delicious food on earth, directly from God, and *free*. Instead of being grateful, they whine: "Manna for breakfast, manna for lunch, manna for dinner . . ." These people sound like your kids at their absolute peak of annoying-ness.

Hearing this complaining, God is angry, but Moses is *finished*. He throws the whole thing back on God in the most fabulous exhausted-leadership tirade of all time:

Moses heard the people weeping throughout their families, all at the entrances of their tents. Then the LORD became very angry, and Moses was displeased. So Moses said to the LORD, "Why have you treated your servant so badly? Why have I not found favor in your sight, that you lay the burden of all this people on me? Did I conceive all this people? Did I give birth to them, that you should say to me, 'Carry them in your bosom, as a nurse carries a sucking child,' to the land that you promised on oath to their ancestors? Where am I to get meat to give to all this people? For they come weeping to me and say, 'Give us meat to eat!' I am not able to carry all this people alone, for they are too heavy for me. If this is the way you are going to treat me, put me to death at once—if I have found favor in your sight—and do not let me see my misery." (vv. 10–15)

Moses is not letting God off the hook on this one. Moses did not want this job in the first place. He had told God that in no uncertain terms. Moses had thought this whole exodus idea was sketchy at best, and he had been very clear about his lack of qualifications for his role. And now *God* is angry? Moses turns on the Lord in fury. *Your people*, who *you* brought out of Egypt. The land that *you* promised them. This whole thing was your idea, and now *I* am stuck breastfeeding this stupid, whiny, impossible people in this dry, desolate, desert place. I don't even know where we are going, and I am supposed to lead them? Just kill me now. Seriously, kill me.

God listens rather quietly until Moses has finished. Then God comes up with a plan. This text is a favorite with community organizers for a reason. God tells Moses to build a team. Leadership will be shared. God will do God's part. Calm down, God tells Moses, it will be OK because you will not be alone anymore.

> So the LORD said to Moses, "Gather for me seventy of the elders of Israel, whom you know to be the elders of the people and officers over them; bring them to the tent of meeting, and have them take their place there with you. I will come down and talk with you there; and I will take some of the spirit that is on you and put it on them; and they shall bear the burden of the people along with you so that you will not bear it all by yourself." (vv. 16–17)

Moses does eventually calm down, after one more testy exchange with God about what the people are going to eat. Moses gets so calm, in fact, that when things go totally out of control and the plan falls apart a minute after it is made, Moses is completely chill.

> So Moses went out and told the people the words of the LORD; and he gathered seventy elders of the people, and placed them all around the tent. Then the LORD came down in the cloud and spoke to him, and took some of the spirit that was on him and put it on the seventy elders; and when the spirit rested upon them, they prophesied. But they did not do so again.

> Two men remained in the camp, one named Eldad, and
> the other named Medad, and the spirit rested on them; they
> were among those registered, but they had not gone out to
> the tent, and so they prophesied in the camp. And a young
> man ran and told Moses, "Eldad and Medad are prophesy-
> ing in the camp." And Joshua son of Nun, the assistant of
> Moses, one of his chosen men, said, "My lord Moses, stop
> them!" But Moses said to him, "Are you jealous for my sake?
> Would that all the Lord's people were prophets, and that
> the LORD would put his spirit on them!" And Moses and the
> elders of Israel returned to the camp. (vv. 24–30)

Moses may have found his happy place, but Joshua is freaking out. And Moses says it will be OK. Better than OK. Really
pretty great actually. Huge. What passes for leadership in a
stressed-out organization can easily become just a chain reac-
tion of people freaking out. What is helpful is when one person
in the room can grab hold of the big picture, if only for a minute. Moses proves the power of his leadership in this moment.
Not long before, he was freaking out himself. But right here, he
gets it. He sees that God is up to something much bigger than
he had realized before.

Joshua looks foolish. To be fair, however, Moses is being pretty
radical. He has just received explicit instructions from God about
how to proceed with leading the exodus, and he takes it all a big
step further without any real divine authorization. He glimpses
a realm of possibility outside the relatively orderly realm of the
tent, a world where the Spirit does what it will, and we all get to
take part.

Moses had tried so hard to lead the people and do God's bid-
ding all on his own that he is ready to see the good news for what
it is. Who the heck are Eldad and Medad? Who knows? We never
find out. We never find out what they did next or what the Spirit
did with them. But there they were for one blazing moment. In
Eldad and Medad, Moses—who had been so afraid that God's
Spirit was too small and too stingy to help him with his problems—
can suddenly see the scope of God's fearsome grace. The Spirit is

everywhere. Everyone can get in on the action. Moses will never carry the whole weight of this people by himself again.

I love this story. For me, it answers the question of what is God up to while we are freaking out and trying to get organized. Spilling the Spirit all over the darn place, that's what. Isn't it glorious?

I wrote my first seminary paper about this passage, in Introduction to Old Testament, with the legendary professor Phyllis Trible at Union Theological Seminary in New York City. I was terrified. I knew almost nothing about the Bible. But I dug in, and this text opened up for me. I kept coming back to the tent: specifically, who is in the tent, and who is out. The structure of the text points again and again to that distinction. One thing is clear. The Spirit of God is everywhere. In. Out. All around. No stopping that messy Spirit from popping up where it will.

Twenty-first-century churches are deeply steeped in assumptions about program and staff and leadership from within. We assume that we will offer new things and others will consume them. We assume it is our job to do things for people. We assume that people will want and expect this from us. When we don't offer the programs church people want, they complain. We live in a tremendously materialistic and consumer-oriented society. We are frequently admonished to do a better job marketing ourselves. We question whether we have anything that the church shopper will want to buy.

One thing about church people (because we are human) is that we want to take credit. I know that from time to time I find myself channeling my inner toddler: "I want to do it *all by myself.* And I want *you* to *watch* me!" Every member of the clergy secretly wants to be that "right leader at the right time" that our bishops and denominational leaders are always talking about. Our congregations mostly have really hard-working leadership; those leaders want to see their efforts pay off. We all want to be the congregation with a clear sense of mission, the church that is making progress because we are doing the right things at the right time. We are supposed to be getting the job done. But what if we don't? What if we can't? This is the next death to which we are called: letting go of needing what happens next to be *ours*. We have believed for so long that for our churches to have life, people will have to come to us.

Time to look outside the tent.

Define the tent however you want. Start small, with the church payroll. Include the lay leadership of the church. Include everyone who comes on Sundays. Include everyone who comes on Christmas and Easter. Include everyone who ever comes. Include everyone who has ever been inside your sanctuary. Make the tent as big as you want, but everyone in the tent has to have something to do with what you are already doing. If you are anything like most churches, you will realize that just about everything you have tried so far—from the raging successes to the embarrassing flops—has been an inside-the-tent job.

So let's take a look outside the tent.

Who's out there in your community? What are they already doing? How can you support them? Can you hope and pray and act for the widest possible reach of the Spirit?

Especially as we come to an end of an era in church economics—one paid pastor, one parish, professionalized clergy, staffed office, and so on—the people outside the tent may be the best news we've gotten yet. Maybe our buildings become the place where people who are ready to do ministry show up and do it. Maybe we don't have to be in control or take credit.

Leading a dying church is not easy, even once things start to get interesting. The people you already have with you—not to mention you yourself—will sometimes get tired and cranky. You're going to need help, and it may be available from some pretty unlikely sources.

What if the Spirit is busy outside the tent, and we just need to give up some of that space we cleared out and let her rip? Wouldn't that be cool?

As long as God's Spirit continues to dwell and move among us, people will be called into ministry, called to serve one another, called to sacrifice themselves, called to give more than they thought they had, called to offer visions and opportunities for wholeness, called to bind up the wounds of the broken and brokenhearted. What if we go out and look for those people and ask what they need? And offer it to the best of our abilities? Could that be the next phase?

At St. Mary's, almost none of the new ministry that has cropped up in our space in recent years could properly be termed as "ours." It is not run by our staff or by long-term leaders of the parish. Much of it happens while no one with longstanding or official institutional connections to the parish is in the building. Even as the rector, involved with keeping the calendar and orienting new users of our space, I find myself surprised when I pop up on Friday evening or some other time when I am not usually at church. The place is hopping. Basketball is going in the parking lot. A forty-kid brass band blasts a whole lot of sound out of the second-story windows. People are cooking in the kitchen and dancing in the courtyard, even praying in the sanctuary. The community garden committee is meeting, and several groups are organizing lobbying trips to Sacramento. *None* of it is ours in the traditional in-the-tent sense. It is our neighbors leading activities for the benefit of their own communities, offering their own talents, their own dreams. Yet it *is* our children's ministry, our community organizing. The church is the community resource that makes space for it to happen, that brings this mix of people together. These are the fruits of making room and saying yes.

What is new and exciting in our ministry depends heavily on people outside the tent. How totally terrifying. How exhilarating. There's never a dull moment, that's for sure.

The burden of carrying a dying church is a heavy one. Most of our churches have committed the error and the sin of refusing to share, of keeping what we have to ourselves, and of doubting our neighbors' capacity to share in leadership. Now we are desperate. Things are at quite a critical point. We would like nothing more than to have someone take some of the burden off of us.

Moses is only able to share leadership because he is beyond desperate. He is not equal to the task, and he is furious with God at leaving him to bear this burden alone. He's ready to hand it off to *anyone*. When Joshua tries to protect the plan, Moses throws caution to the wind. This thing is so heavy, he's convinced that anyone who will take some of the load can have it.

This is the freedom of the dying church. We can turn to people who we would never have turned to in more respectable days. We can throw caution to the wind and invite the most unlikely people to come on in and take over. We can trust that God is profligate with God's Spirit and that is OK, a relief really, because we really are done being the ones in charge, the ones with all the weight in our hands.

This is very, very good news.

In your neighborhood, there are people. Not just any people, but really cool, interesting people. People with vision. People who stand up for what is right. People who want good things for their neighbors and their kids and their neighbors' kids. People who want good things for the world and are willing to work hard to make those good things happen. Quirky, real people, busy people, disorganized people, but people who are absolutely worth knowing. Many of them are not religious. Some are religious in ways that are totally incompatible with your way of being religious. Most of them will never come worship at your church. Some will surprise you.

It's OK. Get out there and find them. Invite them to use your tent. If they don't come, assume the Spirit of God is on the loose out there anyway. Be their friend. Be their ally. Show up. Care about what they care about. Let them meet in your parish hall. Don't charge too much, but do invite them to pitch in with a box of toilet paper and to come to your next cleanup day. Don't give too much advice.

Let no one who genuinely seems to care about what happens next in your little corner of the world be too weird or too out there for you to appreciate them. Assume God's Spirit is out there, slopping generous doses of inspiration and courage and vision in the most unlikely places.

Hand off the burden. If your church has life, someone will be found to carry the load. If not, that's OK too. Maybe the Spirit is busy down the street, and as long as God's sons and daughters are prophesying, all will be well.

One of my favorite pieces of spiritual wisdom lately is a quote that apparently originated in the movie *The Best Exotic Marigold Hotel.* It goes something like this: "All will be well in the end. If all is not well, it must not be the end." This is much better eschatology that what is in the *Left Behind* series. Don't assume you will get to see the end. Be a little hopeful. A little optimistic. A little generous.

Do what would have embarrassed you in middle school. Tell people you want to be their friend. Tell them you need friends. Show them your grubby little treasure collection. Look at their grubby treasures too. Invite them to join your club. Join theirs. It doesn't really matter how you do it or if you end up in the weird kids' group. Weird kids are cool these days.

In every community there are people Jesus would be proud to claim as followers: people who choose love, who give sacrificially, who put the needs of their communities before their own needs, who look fear in the face and choose to walk the life-giving Way. They may or may not have anything to do with church. They may not identify as Christians. They may even be a little grossed out by the whole church thing. When did attendance at worship and involvement in the institutional church become the primary marks of Christians?

Can we look beyond churchiness for holiness? A part of the challenge of getting out there is looking for leaders. Who are the leaders in your community? The Christ-like leaders? How can you meet them? Support them? Ask them for help? Are you building something they recognize as being worth something to the community they love? If not, maybe you need their help in imagining what to build.

It's not about co-opting Christ-like leaders and it's not about taking credit. It's about joining in on what the Spirit is up to, finding ways to love the community alongside the other people who are out there loving it, offering up your resources, becoming a place where God's people have space to spread their wings. For heaven's sake, don't cast yourself as Joshua, looking for a way to stop momentum that comes from outside your congregation. Get out of your tent and thank God that you are not carrying this burden all alone.

Chapter Eight

Expect Trespasses

"But to what will I compare this generation? It is like children sitting in the marketplaces and calling to one another, 'We played the flute for you, and you did not dance; we wailed, and you did not mourn.' For John came neither eating nor drinking, and they say, 'He has a demon'; the Son of Man came eating and drinking, and they say, 'Look, a glutton and a drunkard, a friend of tax collectors and sinners!' Yet wisdom is vindicated by her deeds."

—Matthew 11:16–19

This is not the easiest bit of Scripture. I've scratched my head over it more than once. Here's what I have come up with as I puzzle over what Jesus was talking about. People are hard to please. All of us. Without exception. We are good at finding the flaws in one another and quick to judge other people for not responding to what we think are obvious invitations and cues. When someone does something that we don't expect, we usually blame them, not ourselves, and certainly not the simple fact that we all do things and hear things differently. We are difficult, and that is to be expected. There is also something more, something deeper, something good about living together. If we expect living with one another to be easy or always to conform to our expectations, we will miss it. We will miss wisdom and transcendence and resurrection.

This chapter is about trespasses. Accepting the inevitability of trespasses may seem awfully passive to be considered a spiritual practice. I believe, however, that as you undertake the more active practices you will find that there are certain realities that govern faithful life, certain truths about our nature as human beings that you will not transcend with the best strategic planning or the most creative ministry. It is better to expect these things, to accept them and even find the joy that they may contain, and to approach your ministry in a state of peaceful awareness of the ways they will shape your journey. Trespasses will be a part of your life of faith. The more you meet and engage with your neighbors, the more true this will be.

It is tempting to blame trespasses on the cultural and linguistic gaps among us. If we were all just a little bit more the same, we imagine, we would understand each other better and spend less time stepping on one another's toes. If you are in a multicultural reality, don't be too quick to attribute all trespasses to culture. Walking toward death in the hope of resurrection is not easy anywhere. It would not likely be much easier, even if your challenges were different. If you are in a more homogeneous environment, you would do well to receive some wisdom oft repeated by my friend, the Reverend Dr. Altagracia Perez: "All ministry is multicultural ministry." She's right. Even in congregations where everyone is the same color, speaks the same language, and lives in the same sort of subdivision, there are still gaps. Gaps of generation and experience and family structure. Gaps in luck, health, and security of income. There is no such thing as a place where everyone is the same, where we never have to be mindful and respectful of the differences between us, or where those differences will never manage to trip up our best efforts at ministry.

Let's just agree: there will be trespasses.

Lately I've been paying a lot of attention to what Jesus asks of us in prayer and relationship. I understand the instructions we are given not just in terms of what we are to do but as signs of what God knows about the formation of human community. Sometimes we imagine that God expects churches (and families) to be perfect, but if that were so, why would we have so much instruction about what to do when things go sour?

Trespasses are my favorite thing about the traditional language version of the Lord's Prayer. They are more colorful, more descriptive, and less loaded than sins. They encompass the large and the small, the pesky and the scary—the squashed toe as well as the midnight intruder.

> Forgive us our trespasses as we forgive those who trespass against us.

The more people we have in and around church, and the more varied those people are in their ways of engaging, the more we step on one another. The longer our congregations have gone without incorporating new people, the more sensitive we become to even small incursions into "our" space.

For several years, I offered a Bible study in the Los Angeles County jail for women. The women at Century Regional Detention Facility and I spent some time unpacking the Lord's Prayer together. Trespasses resonated deeply in that context. Several of the women had faced trespassing charges. They also understood exactly how the concept of trespassing applied to living in a small space in a community not of their own choosing. In jail there is no privacy. Strangers learn your intimate habits, hear you snore, watch you pee, hear you cry yourself to sleep. Gossip is rampant. Everyone is stressed out. The incarcerated Bible studiers agreed: when huge things have gone wrong, heavy systems are against you, and serious mistakes have been made, it is often the smallest trespasses that push you over the edge. The more fragile our space is, the more we defend what little space we have managed to carve out.

We so often look to God to defend our point of view. We claim our ways of doing things as orderly and pleasing, even holy. We suspect that other people's ways can lead only to chaos. We post elaborate signs and lists of instructions, imagining that if people only had more information, they would come around to our way of thinking and doing.

As I pray the Lord's Prayer, I see a hint of a smile on God's face. Ah yes, there will be trespasses.

There will be trespasses—then what?

At St. Mary's, we are becoming a center for community activity. Rooms that once stood empty are filled with music, dance, exercise, English classes, community meetings. There are trespasses. People forget to check the schedule; use other people's tablecloths; neglect to take out the trash; spill things that are sticky; put up decorations that others find garish, using tape that damages the paint. Trespasses have stemmed from everything from proper storage of kitchen supplies to the use of incense to personal hygiene, from what level of child rambunctiousness requires removal from church to how many sandwiches is too many on one plate at coffee hour.

The sorts of trespasses that come with growth and change in our churches tend to be relatively small. There's no blood, no weaponry, but the offenses tap deeper anxieties and raise larger questions about what church is for, how best to take care of it, and whether there is space for all of us in it. Trespasses make people genuinely uncomfortable.

> We want things to be orderly, and chaos seems to reign.
> We had a system, and it no longer seems to work.
> We expected one thing and got another.

Trespasses arise even when everyone's intentions are good. I still cringe just a little when I think of the Christmas Festival story. Every year on the last Sunday of Advent, St. Mary's celebrates a slightly early "Christmas Festival." The children perform a pageant during the service, and there is a program of entertainment on the parish hall stage during coffee hour. This beloved tradition predates me by decades, and I have endeavored to do my part in keeping it alive, ignoring the protestations of my Adventpurist colleagues.

Relatively early in the church's relationship with our Oaxacan neighbors, it occurred to me that a shared interest in traditional dance might be a point of connection between St. Mary's

Japanese American community and our newer neighbors. The Japanese classical dance troupe at the church was rehearsing a dance for the Christmas Festival. I suggested that we invite the Oaxacan dancers to perform as well.

The Japanese dance performance was timed down to the second, tightly choreographed to a piece of music that lasted just under three minutes. It was beautiful, quiet, and subtle. It is a "less is more" sort of aesthetic.

Zapotec traditional dance from Oaxaca is also beautiful, but not quiet or subtle. The movements are exuberant and athletic, and the music is loud. I knew this, and planned the program to highlight what I thought would be a pleasing contrast. What I didn't quite know, having only limited personal experience, was that Zapotec dances typically last twenty or thirty minutes. I also didn't quite realize that an invitation to dance at another community's festival was an invitation that meant something well beyond the sort of general good time togetherness I was imagining. Honoring such a request called for a "more is more" response, and our neighboring community had gone all out. I had suggested "a dance or two." The community planned four, bringing dozens of dancers, costume changes, multiple CDs and a live band. There wasn't quite room on the stage for all they had planned.

I wish I could say that we all rallied and just enjoyed one another's offerings, but it was a hard day. Longtime St. Mary's folks were simply not prepared for hours of dancing, especially dancing that was so unfamiliar in style. The Christmas Festival as practiced through the decades lasts an hour at the most. Our Oaxacan neighbors sensed nearly immediately that there was a mismatch between their offering and our expectations. They adapted, but could only stretch so far from what they had prepared. The congregation was fairly patient, but everyone struggled. The contrast between the two offerings of dance served to magnify the cultural gap I had hoped to narrow. Everyone left feeling more than a little stepped on. I felt more than a little crushed.

The following year, around September or so, I received a suggestion that there be a pre-agreed time limit on the length of all dances at parish events. I honestly believe that the suggestion was

meant to be helpful. I also believe that had we invited the dancers back under those conditions, it would have completed the
humiliation of arriving at someone else's party with very much
the wrong sort of gift. As we come together, rules rarely help
very much in heading off trespasses. They often only serve to
highlight the pain of misunderstanding and the sting of being
misunderstood. We moved away from dance at the next year's
Christmas Festival, allowing time to heal and relationships to
build. In another year or two, we might be ready to try again.

No chapter on trespasses would be complete without one story
set in a church kitchen. One Sunday morning, I encountered a
small group of longtime members looking around the kitchen in
dismay. In the grand scheme of things, it was not the worst of
all messes, but there were certainly issues. Someone had tried to
wash a container of pureed beans down the sink, and had suc-
ceeded only in clogging the drain trap and leaving the sink half
full of foul, beany water. The evidence suggested that they had
given up for the time being, and left the rest of their dishes in a
(neat) pile to be washed later. The ladies preparing coffee hour
for our English service were outraged. They wanted to know who
had done such a thing.

I knew more or less who was responsible for the beans. One
of the new communities in the church had had a big event at
another location the day before, and had prepared much of the
food in St. Mary's kitchen. I had been at the event actually, celebrated a mass, eaten some of the offending beans. I knew that
the celebration had gone late; the organizers had been exhausted.
Based on past experience, I was fully confident they would be
back to finish cleaning and organizing before the day was out. I
had a hard time being angry about the mess. I was too busy feeling pleased that the newer members felt at home enough to leave
the kitchen when they were falling-down tired and come back
later. I do it all the time in my own kitchen but would never do it
in a place where I was a guest. I was glad they were getting to the
point where they no longer felt like guests.

Despite my warm feelings, the sink was gross. Worse, the new folks had violated a hard-and-fast old-timer rule at St. Mary's. You don't walk out of the kitchen until it is spotless. There is no later. It doesn't matter how tired you are. Old-time St. Mary's folks live by this rule. And man is that kitchen clean at the end of every event.

Of course this wasn't exactly always true. Back in the days of St. Mary's giant bazaar-carnival, Saturday was game day and Sunday was clean-up time. But in those days, there was no "us" and "them." Everyone was on the same team, and everyone knew what the rules and expectations were. No one showed up on Sunday who hadn't been there the day before. Everyone knew when clean-up time was, and no one expected to find the kitchen clean when clean-up time wasn't over yet.

Faced with the beans and the displeasure, I did the only thing that I could think of to do in the moment. I rolled up my sleeves and cleaned the beans out of the sink. I couldn't just leave them there. Only one of the three usable sinks in the kitchen was clogged, but it was *really* bothering people. It wasn't fair to ask the old-timers to do it, and I wasn't going to make a scolding call to the new folks. I don't know if it was the most helpful approach. The old-timers remained irritated. No open and cathartic discussion of kitchen etiquette ensued. No reconciliation came about. It was not that kind of day. I just made the call that it wasn't really a teaching moment, dug my hand down into the beany soup, and kept digging until the water flowed freely again.

We have choices when there are trespasses. We can let things slide. We can post lists of rules. We can make announcements. We can ask people to change their behavior. We can facilitate tense discussions. We can sit and silently fume. We can limit access. When we find ourselves confronted with choices, it helps if we know where we're trying to go.

- Are we trying to preserve cleanliness? Build community?
- Do we want new people to feel like tenants? Guests? Part of the family?

- What are we willing to give up? What are we willing to offer?

Not all goals are mutually compatible. The easiest way to keep things nice in a church building is almost always limiting access. The fewer people who use the kitchen, the less likely we are to find a mess. The more sign-up sheets and schedules, the more likely we are to know who to pin the mess on. We can hedge our bets with cleaning deposits and on-site staff to conduct inspections.

Or we can moderate our expectations, find a margin of grace. Clean up and soothe our irritation with gratitude for new life. Accept offerings that may not match what we wanted but enjoy them anyway because they were given with good intention.

We have choices. Our choices matter. People are sensitive—new people and old people alike. It is not realistic to think that we will prevent irritation. What we do with the irritation becomes the question. A little humility and a sense of the larger reasons for our and the church's existence go a long way. A little grace. Again and again and again.

> Then Peter came and said to him, "Lord, if another member of the church sins against me, how often should I forgive? As many as seven times?" Jesus said to him, "Not seven times, but, I tell you, seventy-seven times." (Matt. 18:21–22)

Toes will be stepped on. Life in the new country is all about balancing toe safety guidelines, our own responsibility for protective footwear, a little care and caution, and a little willingness to endure a bruise or two for Jesus' sake. A few bandaged toes may be a good sign that we are up to exactly what Jesus hoped we would be up to.

Chapter Nine

When Faith and Hope Fail, Try Love

Just then a lawyer stood up to test Jesus. "Teacher," he said, "what must I do to inherit eternal life?" He said to him, "What is written in the law? What do you read there?" He answered, "You shall love the Lord your God with all your heart, and with all your soul, and with all your strength, and with all your mind; and your neighbor as yourself." And he said to him, "You have given the right answer; do this, and you will live." But wanting to justify himself, he asked Jesus, "And who is my neighbor?"

—Luke 10:25–29

Ah, but wouldn't life have been simpler had the pesky lawyer not asked that last question! He already had the right answer. Getting a right answer in a conversation with Jesus is no small feat. Why couldn't he just leave well enough alone?

Humans—to varying extents based on privilege—are able to choose their neighbors. The old real estate saying, "location, location, location" is all about the importance people place on choosing what sorts of people, businesses, and activity they want close to them. The same house in a "good neighborhood" will be worth several times what it would bring in a "bad neighborhood." People's measures of neighborhood will vary, but demographic data suggest that living near other people of similar race, culture, and economic status is important. The more choices people have by virtue of wealth and freedom of movement, the more likely they are to choose to live with other people much like themselves.

An important part of being a historic church is that you don't get to choose your neighbors. You are stuck. Sure, when your church was founded, someone decided that this was a neighborhood that could use a church of whatever sort your church happens to be. Someone thought this was a good place to be. But chances are, the intervening years have brought changes. Your church may even have seen neighboring churches close or move away. Your church may have considered moving. Mine moved once early on and apparently considered it again thirty or forty years ago. For whatever reason, you didn't move, and neither did we, at least not the second time. Or you did move, and somehow it didn't help as much as you thought it might. And now you are stuck. At this late date most churches are too rooted, too cumbersome, and not nearly nimble enough to move. Most of us are stuck with the neighbors who come and go around us, the people who are close to us not because we chose them or they chose us, but because we have all ended up in the same place for now.

Who is my neighbor? In the language of the New Testament, "neighbor" comes from a Greek word root that just means "close by." It may seem obvious that your neighbors are the people around you, but it's impressive what many of us will do to parse the term—seeking to wiggle out of any commitment to the people around us who don't seem like promising relationship material.

Jesus, of course, does not just answer the question, "Who is my neighbor?" He tells a story, the story widely known as the parable of the Good Samaritan. It's all about the temptation to dodge our neighbors and all their treacherous problems. Just walk on by. Do not cross the street. In his Jesus-y way, he adds a special twist. The despised Samaritan gets to be the hero. The respectable churchy types (well, synagogue-y, in Jesus' context) don't come out looking so good.

But maybe the most important thing Jesus does in the story of the Good Samaritan is turn around the question. Not, "Who is my neighbor?" Rather, "Who was a neighbor?" At the end of the story, Jesus asks,

"Which of these three, do you think, was a neighbor to the man who fell into the hands of the robbers?" [The lawyer who had asked the initial question] said, "The one who showed him mercy." Jesus said to him, "Go and do likewise." (Luke 10:36–37)

Darn that lawyer! He did exactly what you are not supposed to do when you are trying to leave yourself some wiggle room. He took general instructions ("love your neighbor") and turned them into something much more specific. Be a neighbor. Show mercy. Cross the street. Care what happens to other people, including people who your people don't historically get along with. Reach out. Make the first move. Risk being made unclean. Face danger. Spend money.

We, my friends, are on the hook now. Thanks to that show-off lawyer, we have work to do. Our churches have marching orders. We had better roll up our sleeves and cross the street.

This final section of practice is about being the neighbor. We've talked about figuring out who our neighbors are, about beginning the process of meeting them, about making our churches more inviting and being open to relationship-building when our neighbors come to us. But we also have to cross the street. *We* have to get out there. It isn't an easy mission. It won't always go well. But that mouthy lawyer and his insistence on asking one more question left us no choice.

And now faith, hope, and love abide, these three; and the greatest of these is love. (1 Cor. 13:13)

St. Mary's motto, for lack of a better term, is from 1 Corinthians: "Faith, Hope, Love." One of the outdoor murals at St. Mary's interprets this motto in English, Spanish, and Japanese. Instead of "Faith, Hope, Love," though, it says, "Faith, Love, Hope." I will confess that I was a little surprised and more than a little dismayed when I first saw it. I tried to find a way to ask about the odd order without hurting the artists' feelings.

"I notice that love ended up in the middle," I said.

"Yes!" the lead artist replied with a big smile. "That's because it's the most important."

We had done a brief Bible study, the artists and I, so that they would know where the phrase had come from. We read 1 Corinthians 13, which is all about love. They may not have gotten the Biblical order right, but the message had come through. Love is the most important. I remember that every time I look at the wall of the church parking lot.

Love is the most important.

All this successful neighboring is well and good. But what about when it doesn't go well? What about when there are real reasons that you don't get along with your neighbors or that they don't get along with you? What about when your best efforts don't seem to lead anywhere good? What about when your neighbors' best efforts aren't even close to what you were hoping for? What about when everyone behaves a little badly? Or a lot badly? There are times in the process of being neighbors when it is easy to lose hope. It is even possible to lose faith. Then all we have left is love.

You may have noticed that the neighborhood around St. Mary's is called Koreatown, but few of my stories of church and neighborliness include Koreans. I did explain that the neighborhood is majority Latino, which provides a partial explanation for this obvious omission. I also speak fluent Spanish and very little Korean. There's another Episcopal Church in Koreatown, and at some point in the slightly shadowy annals of the past, someone decided that "they would do Korean, and we would do Spanish." Another piece of the puzzle.

All these somewhat reasonable explanations notwithstanding, St. Mary's is in the middle of what is possibly the largest Korean community outside of the Korean peninsula, and we have fairly minimal contact with our Korean neighbors. I can't end a book about churches and neighbors and faithfulness and not talk about that reality. I can't end a book that suggests that we are saved by believing in *resurrection*, of all things, and then say that some things are just too difficult and should better be left alone. God raised Jesus from the *dead*, for heaven's sake. If that was not too impossible to touch, neither should any of our neighbors be too difficult to include in our practice of love and forgiveness.

When my daughter was in preschool, the thing she loved most was being told stories. Her favorite stories were riffs on real things that happened in our lives. I must have told one thousand variations on the story of a minor car accident that she experienced with her father. "Now tell it with me driving the car and my teddy bear sitting in the car seat." "Now tell it when I didn't wear my seatbelt and I got bloody and got dead." I passed on telling that one.

Whenever something interesting happened, my daughter would stop to consider for a moment, maybe ask some questions, then say, "Tell me the story of it."

What is up with St. Mary's and me and the Koreans of Koreatown? I will do my best to tell you the story of it. I will try to be fair to everyone involved. I will mostly tell my part of the story, because that's the part I know best, and have prayed about, and have tried to shape in accordance with my own struggle to be faithful.

I'll start, however, with other people's stories. Here is a vast oversimplification of thousands of years of East Asian history: Japanese and Korean people have spent a long time hating each other's guts. The most recent—and very serious—grievance on the Korean side of this equation has to do with Korea's thirty-plus years as a Japanese colony early in the twentieth century, culminating in a stunning variety of atrocities committed by the Japanese army during World War II. Japan, as a nation, has not done a very good job of taking responsibility or being sorry for these events. Ethnic Koreans living in Japan continue to suffer discrimination and second-class citizen status (or in some cases denial of citizenship despite long family histories in Japan).

You will recall that St. Mary's is a historic Japanese American church, with its own very serious World War II history and its own set of very real grievances and sorrows about World War II-era injustices perpetrated by the government of the United States. St. Mary's members and their ancestors had, with few exceptions, already left Japan by the time the most recent outrages against

Koreans took place. Being held responsible for things that Japan did or does, just because they are ethnically Japanese, opens up an extremely painful set of wounds, harkening back to the suspicions cast on the Japanese American community during World War II.

That's about as far as I will go in trying to portray other people's perspectives on the difficulties of St. Mary's building a loving relationship with its Korean neighbors. Both the events of the past century and historical geopolitics are against us. Hopefully you can see that the situation is not an easy one from any angle. Opportunities abound for mistrust, misunderstanding, oversimplification, overgeneralization, and any number of other unhelpful phenomena.

Into this big-picture mess wanders a white woman priest, called to help St. Mary's turn its energy toward the project of becoming a neighborhood church. What could possibly go wrong?

I actually moved to Koreatown almost ten years before I became the rector at St. Mary's. I moved here voluntarily but not because I had any particular interest in Koreans or Korean culture. In fact, I knew very little about Koreatown. My family wanted a house. We were living in an apartment a few miles to the west of Koreatown. We liked where we lived, but we had a baby, and our once-spacious apartment suddenly seemed small and cluttered with way too much baby stuff. Because we liked where we lived, we started looking for houses around there. It turned out that at the tip-top end of our price range, there were a few houses for sale. They were, without exception, the bottom of the housing barrel. We saw places where the original owner had just died, having performed virtually no maintenance in the last forty years. We saw one house with 6.5-foot ceilings. My husband is almost 6 foot 2 inches. We stepped on large squishy areas of flooring, on the second story of a house carefully covered over with new carpet. We learned about all the things that earthquakes have done to foundations in our part of the city.

The true story of how I ended up living in Koreatown, about a mile and a half north of St. Mary's, is more about housing prices than vocation. At the time we bought our house, prices went down, by half, the minute one crossed Western Avenue (a major north-south thoroughfare) heading east. So we bought a great house east of Western, in a neighborhood with lots of people who had bought a few years earlier, when literal fire-sale prices at the end of the 1992 civil unrest had made the Craftsman houses of Koreatown an incredible bargain. Our immediate neighbors are Filipino, Anglo, and Hawaiian, but there are many Koreans in our neighborhood as well.

This is all to explain that I had had quite a bit of time and opportunity to form an impression of the Korean side of Koreatown by the time I got to St. Mary's. I had already made my own forays and mistakes before I even entered the mix at St. Mary's. One of my daughters attended our neighborhood elementary school in a Korean-English dual language program. Her classmates for those six years were almost exclusively the children of Korean immigrants. Her teachers were all Korean or Korean American. Our whole family learned tae kwon do at a local school run by a Korean grandmaster and a mix of Korean and Latino instructors. We ate a lot of Korean food at local restaurants and began doing more of our shopping at the local Korean supermarkets. I make a mean kimchi fried rice, if I do say so myself.

Living in Koreatown, we learned which places were friendly to non-Koreans and which places not so much. We struggled with elements of the Korean community leadership that seemed to have a vision for carving out all-Korean space, leaving little room and few resources for the many non-Koreans living in the neighborhood. We formed close relationships with the Korean masters and instructors at tae kwon do. Our family never found a comfortable place in the Korean social scene at school, but our daughter loved several of her teachers dearly. It was all a pretty mixed bag. As time went on, I found myself lumping my Korean immigrant neighbors together in my mind more often than I am proud to admit. I quietly agreed with the assessment put forward by more than one of my non-Korean neighbors—that the Koreans of Koreatown were, as a group, tough people to be neighbors with. I dismissed many aspects of Korean culture as impenetrably strange.

When I was called to St. Mary's, it was something of a relief that not much was expected of me on the Korean front. My skills in Spanish and experience in U.S. Latino contexts positioned me relatively well to start building relationships with St. Mary's Latino neighbors. With Korean neighbors, I didn't have much going for me, even without my attitude problems.

Almost right away, however, signs began to emerge that neither I nor St. Mary's was going be let off the hook on engaging all of our neighbors in Koreatown. A proposal for collaboration with a local group of Korean Episcopalians landed on our doorstep months after I started at St. Mary's. The resulting discernment process was a disastrous mix of missed cues, miscommunications, hurt feelings, and general mutual mystification. We were all trying fairly hard, but probably none of us was trying quite hard enough. Whatever assumptions we brought with us about how difficult it might be to work together were more than confirmed by the actual difficulties we encountered.

I decided I was going to have to try to do better. I set out to improve my understanding of my Korean neighbors and my abilities to communicate. I prayed. I asked for help. Reading and learning from Korean American friends and colleagues helped me to understand how deeply wounded the Korean community is by stereotypes and perceptions (even seemingly positive ones) that isolate Koreans and Korean Americans from their neighbors. My own mystification, frustration, and exhaustion at the difficulties of even the simplest interactions with my first-generation immigrant Korean colleagues and neighbors slowly led to a greater compassion for what it must be like to immigrate to a country where none of the ways that you have learned to behave and get things done seem to work the way they should.

I went to Korea. To be honest, I wasn't sure what I would get out of the trip. I outlined some learning goals and questions for the grant that provided funding, but the real reason for going was that I was pretty sure it would change me. It was a pilgrimage much more than a research mission. I was not disappointed. I learned a little bit about Korea and Koreans in my ten days hosted by the Anglican Church in Korea, but I learned (or relearned) a great deal more about myself. An evangelical expression rarely used in my own religious circles best expresses the experience. I came back "convicted." I experienced having the light of the gospel shone on me and being found badly wanting. I came back with new conviction as a Christian and as a human. I remembered the basics about love of neighbor, and I saw how far I had strayed from the Way.

I arrived in Korea with my eleven-year-old daughter in tow and was presented with a full schedule. Nothing was left to chance. One of my Los Angeles Korean colleagues (who sometimes doesn't return my local calls and emails for weeks or months at a time) was in touch daily to make sure that I was both well taken care of and obediently following the schedule. Korean clergy who I had met briefly in Los Angeles, and some I had never met, were detailed to spend entire days shuttling my daughter and me around Seoul and beyond. The archbishop covered all of our lodging expenses (despite knowing that we had funds to cover them) and made time in a very busy week to eat with us and show us things we could not have seen without him.

The hospitality was overwhelming. I thought about the Korean clergy who have been coming to Los Angeles to do chaplaincy internships over the last several years. Their welcome (not unlike the welcome of virtually all immigrants and visitors who arrive in LA) is largely left to members of their own ethnic community. Their interaction with non-Koreans is limited, stressful, and burdened by language barriers and cultural awkwardness. When in Korea we arrived to spend the night at the home of a friend of a colleague, our hostess was shocked (and maybe a little horrified) to discover that the "friends from LA" were not Koreans. Nothing in her own experience of the U.S., where she had lived for several years, suggested that non-Korean Americans were available for friendship. I returned from Korea deeply aware of the contrast between the hospitality we received and the fend-for-yourself approach that visitors and immigrants to the U.S. experience.

In Korea, I experienced my Korean colleagues on their home turf. One priest who hosted us for two days was someone I had only met relatively briefly in Los Angeles. In LA, my impression of her had been of someone who was tiny (we are more than a foot apart in height), quiet, and deferential. When she summoned us out of a crowd in the Busan train station, she actually seemed taller. She spoke loudly and with confidence, scolding us for various oversights and fussing over us like a mother hen. I discovered in conversation that her English was excellent, which turned out to be rather easily explained by five years studying at Oxford. In LA, I had never had a complex conversation with her or bothered to inquire about her background. She had commandeered a parade of friends to take us out to eat, keep us overnight, and show us around Busan. An additional parade of friends, hearing she was in town, popped up to greet her as we made our way. In addition to being a priest, she was part of the first wave of women to graduate from pharmacy school in Korea, and these were her fellow pioneers. When she arranged for a dinner with other women clergy, I discovered her as matriarch, listening to each younger woman's troubles in turn, dispensing advice and ending the evening by sending everyone home with a small gift of a clergy collar tab. Her foreignness had diminished her in my Los Angeles eyes. Her home country, and my less sanguine position as visitor, revealed much that I had failed to see.

I returned from Korea remembering that Jesus turns the question back on the lawyer. Not, "who is my neighbor?" but "who was a neighbor?" All the time and energy I had spent searching for ways to make Koreans into better or more understandable neighbor material turned back on me and revealed my own call to be the neighbor. I returned from Korea having relearned a lesson of my cross-cultural childhood: that without the shortcut of words and mutual language, relationships blossom differently, more slowly, with greater effort but with unique beauty nonetheless. In Korea, I found that the first two or three hours of a long day with a fellow priest who spoke limited English (but always much more English than I speak Korean) were often excruciating for everyone involved. But the last three or four hours could be awesome, full of real questions and heartfelt explanations punctuated by hovering together over smartphone translators and laughing at our misunderstandings. I realized that I had rarely gotten beyond the first few awkward minutes before giving up on relationship building with my Korean colleagues and neighbors in Los Angeles. Starting with my colleagues and the visiting clergy, I have begun—little by little—to work at being a better neighbor.

One piece of the neighboring project is my attempt to learn some Korean, with the help of a patient and generous Korean friend. It isn't easy. I have my doubts about whether my Korean skills will ever equal even the most basic English that my immigrant neighbors can manage. So far, the benefits of my study have mostly been shifts in perspective. When I find myself gulping back tears of frustration after a simple workbook listening exercise in which I have once again understood nothing, I begin to understand why many of my Korean neighbors retreat from opportunities to "practice their English." When my weak attempts to communicate in Korean with a few friendly colleagues are rewarded with warm smiles and words of encouragement, I am acutely aware of the much chillier reception that Korean-accented English receives in most quarters of LA. As I puzzle over all the complex social information contained in Korean verbs, I imagine my neighbors trying to show and perceive respect in English, whose verbs tell you next to nothing about the relationship between speaker and hearer.

My efforts to be a better neighbor in Koreatown are a work in progress. I backslide. I'm sure that I still offend my Korean colleagues on a fairly regular basis, but they seem to give me a pretty wide margin of grace. To be fair, they still drive me nuts too on occasion, but I have learned more about what to expect. I try to imagine good things about what they are trying to do and to communicate, and I hope that they do the same for me. On my best days, I start from a posture of repentance—recognizing how deeply I am a part of the brokenness of the community where I live and serve, and looking for ways that God might be calling all of us toward wholeness.

You may or may not find yourself with any neighbors where the cultural and linguistic gaps are as large as they are between me,

St. Mary's, and our Korean neighbors. But there will no doubt be moments when you wonder whether your neighbors are worth the trouble. There will be moments when it seems that your neighbors have decided that you and your congregation are definitely *not* worth the trouble. There will be things that you will not understand, even if you puzzle, like Dr. Seuss's Grinch, "until your puzzler is sore."

At those moments, turn around the question. Try approaching the layers of misunderstanding heart-first, not head-first. Seek creative ways to invite your neighbors to do the same with you. Imagine that you may seem just as difficult, your ways just as impenetrable. Imagine that because your church was there first, you actually may have an easier time than the newer arrivals in this new territory of your neighborhood. Imagine that you might not be called to judge. Imagine that your only call might be to love. If you have lost hope for a future with your neighbors and are struggling to hold on to the faith that your neighbors are worth dealing with, try love. It's in the middle of the mural because it's the most important.

Conclusion

There's no place in this world where I'll belong when
  I'm gone
And I won't know the right from the wrong when I'm
  gone
And you won't find me singin' on this song when I'm
  gone
So I guess I'll have to do it while I'm here

—Phil Ochs[1]

I am going to finish pretty much right where I started: in the middle of it all. I don't know what is going to happen to my own dying church, much less to yours. Every cool experiment and moment of hope at St. Mary's is balanced by clear and convincing evidence that death is nearer now than when we started. I can't share all that evidence, because much of it comes in the form of stories about real people and real losses that are still far too raw to touch and not entirely mine to share. I suspect I don't need to tell you those stories because you have your own stories, your own losses to grapple with, your own clear and convincing evidence weighing in.

1. Phil Ochs, "When I'm Gone," *Phil Ochs in Concert*, 1966, Elektra Records, 33rpm.

At this writing, the wider church is still working at denying its own mortality. Death is defied, denied, and demeaned. If nothing else, I hope I have convinced you that staring down death or running in the other direction is a lost cause. I hope I have given you permission to read the writing on the wall, to see the signs of the times, and to know that you are not crazy when you perceive that very soon nothing will be the same in your church or most others.

I also hope to have convinced you that there is reason to be wildly, irrationally, exuberantly hopeful. Given even the tiniest smidgen of space, the Holy Spirit makes new things happen. They may not be the things you were waiting for, or even the things you were hoping for, but they are new in the way that only things that come from God can be new. The newness comes in ways that are not always easy to see up close.

I find parish ministry to be like walking the labyrinth. Labyrinths are not mazes, requiring guesswork and strategy, but paths, winding to a quiet center, then back out again, usually the way you came. Sitting in the middle of a spectacular outdoor labyrinth recently, I had an easy view of the book and sweatshirt I had left at the entrance. Three or four long-legged strides would have taken me out of the circle, back to my stuff. As I sat in the center, though, I could feel the distance between me and my small pile of discarded things. I had traveled from them, and the proper way back would involve more travel still. Parish ministry, not so different from the Benedictine enclosure, leaves us wandering limited geography, often in full view of where we started. Taking stock of God's movement in the parish's life, and in ours, requires a sense of distance traveled within confined space. Not linear but circular, circuitous, doubling back and retracing steps, noticing different details each time, subtly reshaping the paths with our own footsteps.

As you wander your limited geography, celebrate the glimpses of God's kingdom that you encounter along the way. Taste the freedom that you were missing when you were still convinced it was your job to keep the church alive. Take risks and let your imagination run wild. You can grieve your losses freely now because you no longer have to pretend that there are no losses.

As Christians we live between acknowledging the power of death and proclaiming the victory of love. The resurrection would not be a big deal if death were just an illusion. Once, early in my ordained ministry, I co-officiated a funeral with a pastor who kept referring to the deceased as having "made the transition." He couldn't seem to bring himself to say that the man was dead. Christian theologies that deny death have that sort of "truthiness" that comedian and political commentator Stephen Colbert named so well. They get close to the truth: that death does not have ultimate power over us. At the same time, they obscure the truth. One look at the face of a grieving family member alleviates any illusion that death is not real and permanent for as far as we humans are able to see. Death devastates. Its sting never goes away. We don't stop missing the people we have lost, and we are never off the hook for caring for the people around us in their grief.

Even as we acknowledge death, we are called to imagine our way beyond it, to believe that we can die and also live forever. Being quite a few years younger than her older sister, my second daughter hears a lot of stories about the time before she joined the family. At some point in her preschool years we could see her beginning to grasp the concept of a time before her own life. "So before I was alive, was I dead?" she wondered. My first instinct was to rush to assure her that no, she wasn't dead. For me even to think of her as dead was terrifying. But before I spoke, I realized that *she* wasn't afraid. She was just convinced that her own existence was larger than the time limits that family stories assigned to it. Hers was a remarkably un-scary take on death. It's where we are when we're not here. Life as we know it is temporary; we will all spend more time dead than alive.

> When we've been there ten thousand years
> Bright shining as the sun
> We've no less days to sing God's praise
> Than when we'd first begun.
> ("Amazing Grace")[2]

2. Richard Broaddus and Andrew Broaddus, "Amazing Grace," *A Collection of Sacred Ballads*, 1790.

I read a dying church story recently that captured my imagination. A dead church story, really. A congregation on the East Coast had declined to the point of closure. Church officials held a meeting for neighbors to talk about what they would like to see done with the property and resources left behind. What caught my attention was that the neighbors said that they would like to see this place remain a church. It wasn't because they wanted a place to *go* to church themselves. That did not seem to be it at all. In fact, these were arguably the exact people whose lack of church participation had occasioned the closure to begin with. They wanted to have a church in their neighborhood because they had a sense that having a church there would add something good.

A good church is a pretty great thing to have in your neighborhood. A place that exists for healing, transformation, bringing people together, putting things in perspective, honoring the heck out of the sacred in all of us and turning the mundane holy? Churches are cool. Who wouldn't want one?

The good news from that angle is that just about every neighborhood in the U.S. already has one. Or five or six or more. We don't all quite live up to that lofty description. But maybe we could. If we loosen our grasp, abandon fear, and give over all we have left, who knows what God might be able to come up with? I muddle along in the faith that what I can ask and imagine for the future of church is but a fraction of what could be.

We are called to ministry in the era of dying church. That much is sure. There is no return to previous eras, though we might well have something to learn from each era of thriving and struggle. All we can do now is walk toward death trusting that what is truly alive and truly holy in who we are will not be consumed.

This mortal life may be temporary, but it is a gift without price. Now is the time to do what is most fun and most important and most life-giving and most loving and most authentic. Rejoice in the people who are with you. Be gentle, knowing that we all take the gut punch of grief from different angles and to different effects. Make the most of who you are and what you have, even if it is only a falling down building and a motley crew of Sunday regulars.

Use your imagination for good. I can't stress this enough as a spiritual practice. We really do have a choice most of the time. We can imagine all that could go wrong, or we can imagine acres of possibility: gardens where there once were weeds, murals covering cinderblock walls, tubas in the basement, food for a hundred bubbling on the kitchen stove. We can imagine that we (or someone else) might screw it all up, or we can imagine that God might accept our small offerings and create something wonderful. Our imaginations usually give us too much credit and God not enough. Who are we mortals to be able to screw something up completely when God is at work making something new?

Make room.
Map the terrain.
Turn out your pockets.
Make pilgrimage.
Try things.
Say yes.
Look outside the tent.
Expect trespasses.
When faith and hope fail, try love.

All of us go down to the dust;
yet even at the grave we make our song:
Alleluia, alleluia, alleluia.
                    (Book of Common Prayer,
                        Burial Service Rite II)[3]

3. *The Book of Common Prayer* (New York: Church Publishing Inc., 1986).